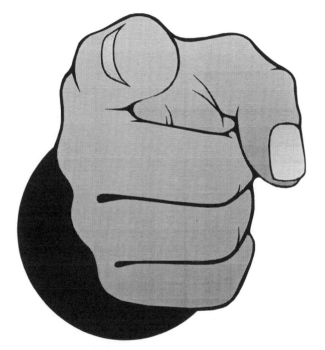

BEHAVIOUR SELF!!

by
Dave Hingsburger

Diverse City Press Inc. (La Presse Divers Cité Inc.)
BM 272, 33 des Floralies
Eastman, Québec
J0E 1P0   (514) 297-3080

LITHO CANADA   **Métrolitho** Sherbrooke (Québec)

Hingsburger, David J.

Behaviour Self: Using Behavioural Concepts to
Understand and Work With People with
Developmental Disabilities

1.   Developmental disability -- problem behaviours
2.   Developmental disability -- behaviour therapy
3.   Behaviour therapy

ISBN 1-896230-06-7

TABLE OF CONTENTS

This book is dedicated to
York Behaviour Management Services,
its director,
Susan Tough,
and all employees, past and present.

Behaviour Management Services has provided me with a place to work, a team that supports, opportunities for growth and an incredible opportunity to provide service in a region fully dedicated to enhancing the lives of people with disabilities. Susan, personally, has given me perspective when I needed it and support when necessary. As a group they have always left the light on for me, and guys, I really do appreciate it.

I would also like to thank *Diverse City Press* and in particular *Joe Jobes* who edited the manuscript and provided insightful suggestions (although they seemed needlessly nitpicky at the time).

Too, my work has been profoundly affected by *Mouth: the voice of disability rights* and, in particular, *Lucy Gwin* who has become a moral sounding board for me.

The *Roeher Institute*, particularly *Roslyn Ward* and *Miriam Ticoll*. Since I moved to Quebec, I have found their openness and willingness to help incredible. Canada is lucky to have you folks.

And *Miss Jean MacQueen* who was the first person to teach me that it is possible to discipline with love and expect with compassion. I owe her much.

INTRODUCTION
A TRANSLATOR'S DICTIONARY

One of the most important tools that one has when wanting to travel to another land wherein people speak a different language, is a small pocket dictionary. These dictionaries give the traveller a serviceable fluency in another language. I know from my move to Quebec that the pages of my dictionary that have allowed me to say the following phrases ...

Excusez-moi, où est le bar?

Une bière, s'il vous plaît?

Une autre, s'il vous plaît?

Avez-vous des beer nuts?

Où est la toilette?

Une bière, s'il vous plaît?

Avez-vous des pretzels?

... are almost worn out!

In the spirit of this book, which suggests that people with developmental disabilities who live within systems created to serve them (isn't that a cute way of putting it?) use their behaviour to communicate feelings, wants and ideas, I offer the following dictionary for your usage. Clearly if we are going to do this work we need to have some idea as to what the behaviour is "saying." This dictionary translates from both the "language" of a person with a disability and a care provider.

Behavioural Language of Person with a Disability

English language translation of Behavioural Language

Hitting out

I want control.

Spitting out food

I want control.

Kicking the furniture

I want control.

Swearing at staff

I want control.

Face slapping

I want control.

Refusing to participate

I want control.

Now, from CPL (Care Provider Lingo) to English

Care Provider Lingo

English language translation of Care Provider Lingo

I am concerned about your behaviour.

I want control.

This programme is for your own good.

I want control.

You need to learn to be appropriate.

I want control.

Locking you into time out is helping you.

I want control.

I'm sorry but because of your behaviour you have lost your community outings, family visits, favourite foods, favourite television programmes, access to your bank account, visits from your boyfriend, access to an advocate, the right to vote at house meetings, access to the telephone, all of your civil liberties and any personal dignity you have left.

I have control.

HARD QUESTIONS

"A referral for who?! She did WHAT!!?"

I will admit to shock. At the weekly meeting reviewing the referrals and the wait list, I couldn't believe my ears when I heard Tracy's name. I saw her quite regularly when I consulted at the sheltered industry. My work there had been done for several months, but I still remembered Tracy and most of the other workers there. She was a quiet and placid young woman who seemed diligent in her work and diffident in her manner. Now I was sitting in a meeting and hearing that she had become violent. She was turning over tables, breaking contract work and being generally a (sound effects ... drum roll ...) behaviour problem. This was not possible, people don't change that much that fast.

Given permission to do a consultation, I set an appointment and went to see the workshop supervisor. She was a wonderful woman who I liked enormously. She greeted me pleasantly and led me into her office. She told me that Tracy was out of control. She was destroying everything in sight. They had segregated her to a part of the workshop where she could get maximum attention and do minimum damage. I asked to go and see her. When I found her in the corner distractedly destroying work that only months ago I had seen her perform in earnest, I was concerned.

One of the rules of our department was that when

any behaviour comes out of the blue, a medical check has to be done. After a few questions, it was clear that we would have to follow this procedure. The supervisor had called in the line staff and our discussion ranged from anger at being hurt to concern for Tracy as she was obviously distraught. Being told that Tracy had come in one day a few weeks before and started acting peculiarly and that there was no known cause for the behaviour, I suggested that the family be contacted and a medical check be done, then we could start working on the problem.

The family reacted poorly to the request. They were understandably upset that the agency had contacted a behaviourist before conferring with them. More than that they felt that some total stranger had no right to give advice or make requests about their child. A territorial fight ensued and as is often the case the battleground was the client's body. After a very difficult day with Tracy wherein her behaviour moved from destruction to outright aggression she was suspended from work and her family was told that she could not come back until the medical check was done and a meeting held with me, the problem causing behaviour therapist.

(Before going on, I do want to say that at the time of this consultation I thought that the problem was the parents. With time and distance I realize that the problem was not the parents; the problem was me. The family was quite right, a total stranger had no right making demands. The family was also right in that they should have been fully informed regarding their daughter's behaviour. They had noted changes too, but thought that she was just upset at home as they had never been informed about the change in their daughter's behaviour at the workshop. Parents have a right to be informed when their child's behaviour changes drastically.)

It didn't take long for the family to capitulate. (Let's face it, we really do hold all the cards.) They took Tracy to the doctor. It can't have been easy for the doctor as Tracy did not communicate using traditional or standard patterns. (I refuse to use the words, "non-communicative" or "non-verbal" except in sentences like this one.) Even so the doctor discovered that Tracy had otitis media, a very painful ear infection. It was felt that perhaps the change in Tracy's behaviour was due to the pain she was experiencing. She was placed on medication to deal with the infection and reduce the pain.

It wasn't long until Tracy was back to herself. Back to work, back to producing, back to smiling. The problem was solved.

THE TRACY DILEMMA

Tracy offers us an interesting question. That is, "What if we had just gone ahead and tried to program her while she was in pain?" Well, let's consider the question. Do you think that we could have programmed away Tracy's behaviours while she was in pain? If you answered "yes" you would unfortunately be right. Take an honest look at Tracy's life. She lives at home with two very powerful people, her parents. She works at a sheltered industry for another very powerful person, her staff. If a meeting were called, not only would these powerful people be there, everyone she knows who has power over her would all come at an agreed upon time to an agreed upon place to talk about her. (A daunting thought!) At this meeting it would be determined that Tracy was a behaviour problem and that she needs some form of behavioural programming.

These powerful people would discuss how to alter all of her environments in order to bring her "tantrum" behaviour under control. They may discuss her food, her activities, her social time, her leisure time, her bed time, her comforts, her stressors, her likes, her dislikes. Once they had categorized these things they would very simply, manipulate them in order to get her to do what they wanted, which would be to sit down, shut up and ignore her own pain. They would ask her to produce when in pain the same amount that she did without pain. They would ask her to interact when in pain in the same way that she did without pain. And Tracy would learn that no one around her cared that she hurt, they only cared that she "did what she was told, when she was told, without question or comment." And Tracy would. These people have incredible power and she would be taught to put up with pain.

At the end of the program, Tracy may have lost all hearing because of the intensity of the infection, she may have learned to endure chronic pain, but she would not be a behaviour problem. The dilemma that behaviourists face is the fact that behavioural programming can work even if the hypothesis for the behaviour is wrong. The people at the table may have determined that Tracy was doing what she was doing because she was seeking attention or avoiding a task. No matter what they thought, the fact that their program worked would lead to an assumption that the right hypothesis was made.

This scene is terrifying because of what could have happened. Tracy was lucky that she was not forced to submit to inhumane programming. Others aren't so lucky, let's look at a slightly different situation. Fred's behaviour changed. Drastically. Quickly. Without explanation. His skills at home and at work decreased by the day. Medical examinations showed no reason for his behaviour to change. The first sign of a problem was when he got up in the morning and refused to get on the bus. This refusal was met with a demand, the demand was met with a tantrum. The staff backed off quickly, realizing that Fred was not typically "a behaviour problem." They assumed that he had just got up on the wrong side of the bed. Fred was asked if he wanted to calm down and then the staff would drive him into work. Fred readily agreed and calmed down considerably. The bus driver was informed that Fred wouldn't be on the bus that morning. Fred was driven into work by the staff.

The following morning, Fred threw a tantrum again when the staff insisted that Fred take the bus. When he refused the staff tried to force him onto the bus. The staff reported that "I felt like I had reinforced inappropriate behaviour by taking him into work the day before." Even with the concern about reinforcing this kind of behaviour, Fred ended up in the staff's car again. Soon there were accusations. Staff at home accused staff at work for changing things to upset Fred. Staff at work stated that nothing had changed except that Fred arrived at work upset, clearly the group home was at fault. A few more calls like this led to a meeting. A meeting led to a definition of the problem. The definition of the problem led to a solution. A solution led to a behaviour program.

Fred would receive reinforcement (access to privileges) for getting on the bus and punishment (denial of privileges) for not getting on the bus. Over time the program began to work. By sheer chance someone who knew Fred and the situation discovered that the bus that Fred took to work took an "unauthorized" stop wherein Fred was being sexually assaulted on the bus by the bus driver.

Fred's behaviour, like Tracy's, was a result of something happening that was outside of his control. Tracy couldn't speak in traditional ways and Fred was experiencing the unspeakable. Both made desperate attempts to tell those around them that something was very wrong. No one listened.

Behaviour programming at its best teaches people with disabilities new skills with which to *control* their own lives. Behaviour programming at its worst takes *control* of someone else's life. Behaviourism has been bashed about a lot because some have come to see it as the problem. Behaviourism has never been the problem, the need for control of some of those who use it has been the problem. And let's face, it most behaviourists face situations where staff, agencies, funding bodies, advocate groups are demanding that they use their skills to bring someone's behaviour under control at any cost -- moral and ethical -- but financial.

My first brushes with behaviourism happened first in an institution in British Columbia, followed by work in an institution in Ontario. In Victoria, I worked at a small institution and was hired to work on the behaviour ward. Not because I had skill but because I was big. It was made very clear that we were not there to teach we were there to control. A successful day was a day wherein everyone sat about in a comatose calm. An unsuccessful day was a day wherein a client's behaviour would cause us to come into some kind of contact with them. Oh, we had our outings and walks, but these were a kind of herding. While working there, I met a young fellow who had enormous behaviour outbursts that were legendary. I watched him and it seemed to me that his inability to communicate, together with his poor vision combined to make the world a frustrating place for him to live.

Even though he "was not my client" I decided that I wanted to give him a means of communicating. I set about using some very large pictures and taught him to point to the picture when he wanted food or drink. These pictures were then placed on the wall, and slowly the wall was turning into a very large picture board where he could ask for things as varied as food and walks. The progress was quick and remarkable. Using behaviour programming to teach him a new sign and then using reinforcement to maintain his communication was easy and fun. I was thrilled. Foolishly, I thought I had done well.

One Monday coming in after a weekend off, I found that all the pictures had been ripped off the walls and he had been in time out for hours. He had had several PRN's to calm him. None had worked. I was called into a meeting where there were a number of high powered professionals along with the female staff who owned Scot. He was "her client" and she confronted me in the meeting saying that she had allowed the programming to go on even though she "knew it would only cause problems." I was confused and when I asked for clarification I discovered that Scot had had an outburst that weekend. "See," I was told, "Your program didn't work; he still has outbursts." Then I was informed that the program had been terminated as unsuccessful and I was forbidden to teach him any new words or to replace the words on the wall.

I tried to convince them that my "program" had nothing to do with outbursts, it was simply aimed at giving him a means of communicating. They surely could see that the program had successfully taught him a number of words that he could communicate with ease and effectiveness. They could not hear me. The program would stop and the program did stop. It was clear that they had no difficulty using behaviour programming to take power but refused to use it to give power.

Years later I would visit that institution to give a workshop. I found that Scot was one of the few that had not been moved. His behaviour had kept him confined physically. His lack of any traditional, respected means of communication had kept him confined spiritually.

MINNIE PRIDE!!!

I was riding the bus with a friend. We were staff at

a small prevocational centre for people with disabilities. We somehow felt pride at going to work at a place where people did meaningless tasks for no pay in preparation for a life where they did meaningless tasks for practically no pay. Even so the harsh glare of reality had yet to hit us in our rush to work. While on the bus a young woman with Down's Syndrome got on. She was dressed, I thought beautifully. She wore a bright clean tee shirt with jeans that matched the tee shirt. She took an empty seat placed her purse into her lap and looked out the window.

My seatmate whispered to me in disgust, "Look at that, who'd let someone go out dressed like that?" I figured I missed something so I looked a little closer. As I was looking, a "youth" got on the bus and took the only remaining seat which was beside the woman in question. He wore dirty jeans torn at the knee, a ripped singlet that allowed us to see a tattoo of a woman with very painful looking swollen breasts. His leather jacket had both arms ripped off and a chain haphazardly sewn around the left arm hole. His left ear was pierced with a small bone. His hair was shaved off and there was a little tattoo of a skull and cross bones above his right ear. It took a force of absolute will to look again at the woman with a disability.

She glanced at her seat partner, smiled, and looked again out the window. She wore a clean tee shirt with Minnie Mouse proudly standing wearing the latest in Minnie fashion, yellow shoes and a bright read polka dot dress. To match the tee shirt the woman had chosen red jeans and black shoes. She also wore a black belt that cinched in her waist. She looked great I thought. I said as much to my seatmate who looked at me in horror. She pointed out to me that everyone was staring at the women with a disability because of her tee shirt it was AGE INAPPROPRIATE. I thought that my seatmate had been blinded in one eye and I asked her if she noticed the young man who sat on the bus beside the woman in question. She said that she hadn't particularly. I suggested that the people on the bus were noticing him not her. She seemed to think that would be OK. We dropped the subject.

Arriving at work we got our morning caffeine laced drinks and joined the other staff discussing our days. She recounted with horror seeing this woman on the bus wearing the tee shirt. Another staff knew her and told us all that this woman had a permanent job making minimum wage working at a (gasp) children's library stocking books and sometimes helping out in the daycare reading books to children. Instead of reacting with glee that this woman had a job with purpose that paid real money, it was decided that those around her had demeaned her. The perfect evidence of this was her tee shirt. When I asked what they would do about it I was told that she would be put "on a behaviour program" that taught her how to choose clothing. I asked what would happen if she still chose Minnie, they told me that they would probably have to use some kind of punishing procedure so that she would pair punishment with the tee shirt.

To this day people believe that behaviour pro-gramming can and should be used to eradicate difference and to make people with disabilities do as they are bidden by those with power. To this day people believe that the woman on the bus had no right to be noticed and the young man could wear clothing that demanded to be noticed. To this day people believe that we can and should program away all evidence of disability. To this day we use behaviour programming as a political tool to take all semblance of free will and free choice away from people with disabilities. To this day hatred of disability infiltrates into the attitudes of those who work in the field of disabilities. To this day people see society's attitude of horror in reaction to a person with a noticeable disability as resulting from the person's expression of disability rather than from bigotry.

POINTS TO CONSIDER

A number of issues need to be clearly stated at the beginning of a book on behaviour techniques and approaches to changing someone else's behaviour.

1) All behaviour communicates and as such behaviourists or those who wish to use behaviourism must see behaviour as a legitimate language that needs decoding.

2) Anyone who attempts to program away a behaviour without understanding its meaning is unethical. We don't need to be right, but we need to have tried to interpret the language.

3) Behaviour programming when successful should leave the client in more control of their lives, not just their behaviour.

4) Behaviour programming when unsuccessful should blame the hypothesis not the client or staff.

5) People with disabilities are complex people, just like those without disabilities, and as such will require a broad palate of services from art therapy to play therapy to psychoanalysis. Behaviour therapy is not always the treatment of choice.

6) Medication is not an evil thing. Like behaviour therapy, it should not be used to control a person but to assist them with control. Since some people without disabilities benefit from appropriate medication so will some people with disabilities.

7) A person who uses behaviour approaches will soon see that the behaviour often communicates about an inappropriate environment or inappropriate treatment. As such the therapist will become, very quickly and often very radically, an advocate.

8) There can be no one philosophy that determines how a diversity of people live. Using behaviour technology to eradicate personal difference and personal choice is an Aryan concept that is very scary.

SUMMARY

I had been attending the United Church in Magog for about a year when I first heard of her. She had been coming to the church for a couple hours a week for over a year, her job was to fold the church bulletin and place any inserts into the folded bulletin. She has a severe disability so it took her teacher much time and patience to teach her the skills. When I learned that a woman with a disability helped to make worship possible I suggested that she be invited to hand out the bulletins one Sunday so that she could see the importance of her work and so that the congregation could meet our most faithful volunteer.

She came on anniversary Sunday. This is one of the days that the church is especially full. Janet stood beside her instructor at the back of the church ready to hand out bulletins. She seemed a bit confused and I watched her watch her staff looking for a cue as to why she was standing at the back of an empty church. I settled myself down into a pew and watched. I didn't have to pass by Janet and her instructor because I had dropped some baked goods off for the lunch after service and had come in through the door from the hall at the front of the sanctuary.

When the first person came in, the instructor gave Janet a bulletin and indicated that she was to give it to the person standing in front of her. Janet took the bulletin and held on to it with all her might. Her face darkened. You could see her thoughts on her face. She had worked hard to fold these, she had piled them carefully and stacked them with pride. There was simply no way that she was going to give one of these to this stranger in front of her. Her instructor nudged her gently and again indicated that she was to give it to the woman in front of her. This Janet did begrudgingly, thrusting it forward in defiance. The woman took it smiled and said something that I could not hear. Janet paused, looked closely at the woman and then tentatively returned her smile.

The next person came in and Janet only had to be instructed once to give the bulletin. Again a smile and a couple of words, but this time Janet brightened and smiled right back, a big, bold beautiful grin. She understood now. Person after person came in and Janet was given a bulletin each time. Her hand now anticipated that coming bulletin and she would reach for it often before the instructor had a chance to get one out. Bulletins flew out of her hand and the smile never had a chance to leave her face as people were coming in a steady stream.

I looked hard at the instructor and tried to will her into just giving Janet the pile. This did not work and being that I was in a church I thought maybe I could do a "bank shot prayer" by bouncing a prayer off heaven's floor back down to the instructor. "Give Janet the pile. Give Janet the pile. Give Janet the pile." Prayer after prayer soared upwards. My aim was poor. The prayer went up hit the floor and bounced down and hit Janet. She grabbed the pile from the instructor and quite independently handed out bulletins to people as they came in. The instructor quietly stepped back a bit and let the limelight shine completely on Janet's accomplishment and participation.

As people were in their seats and only latecomers were arriving, Janet began to look around and see all the people in the church looking at the bulletins for the order of service. Then a straggler arrived and Janet took the bulletin and handed it to him. He stood for a minute and said something to her. Janet doesn't speak using traditional messages, but she desperately wanted to answer the man. She took the bulletins held them to her chest with one hand and then tapped her chest. This is a woman who has given up on communication and the word I saw her say was "Me!" The sentence I heard her say was, "Me, I did this!" The sentiment I heard her say was, "ME ... I'm proud of me!"

Using traditional methods of teaching Janet slowly had learned how to fold. Praise taught her the skill. Many trials, many errors, many triumphs and she learned the skill. But there in the church she became a single trial learner as she experienced the most important reinforcer of all ... respectful human interaction.

Behaviour therapy at its best goes from teaching a skill to changing a life.

WAIT A MINUTE ...

Some of you just thought to yourself that what I have described is not behaviour therapy. Well, actually it is. The teaching process used to teach Janet involved a task analysis, the use of scheduled reinforcers and a fading procedure that enabled the teacher to reduce the prompts necessary for her to do the task independently. This is behaviour therapy. I have always thought that the word "therapy" was a misnomer because the best and most ethical behaviour approaches involve teaching skills not uncovering neurosis.

2

WHAT'S GOING ON HERE?

Once in northern B.C. on a lecture tour, I came down with a very severe throat infection and by the ache in my ear I suspected the infection had spread. This is an extremely difficult problem for a lecturer because I was going to need my voice to get through several days of training that had been scheduled for months. Luckily I was travelling with my friend Linda and she pushed me into a car and took me off to the emergency room at the hospital.

We drove right across town taking a good, oh, two, three minutes and took one of the four spaces in the hospital parking lot. We went in and found an empty emergency room. Wandering about and calling into various rooms we finally found the receptionist taking a smoke break out across the road. She quickly butted out and came back inside the hospital. With a great deal of drama and self importance she sat down at her desk, rearranged a few things and then looked up at us like we had just arrived. "May I help you?"

I told her that I needed to see a doctor as I suspected I needed a prescription for antibiotics. She told me that there was no doctor on duty. When I looked confused, she asked me if I would like her to phone one of the doctors at their offices and make an appointment for me. I asked why there were no doctors in the emergency room and she told me that they "weren't anticipating any emergencies." Oh. She made an appointment for me with a local doctor and gave us directions so that we could take our unanticipated emergency out of her face.

Linda got me back into the car and drove to the address given us by the nurse. When we arrived, I gave my name and particulars and was instructed to take a seat. The seats in the waiting room were all those barbaric chairs with little tiny seats and hard metal arms. I don't fit into those chairs so I didn't even try. Twice I was told to sit, twice I said, "No thanks." I am firmly convinced that thin people are either blind or suffer from a deep seated nastiness brought about by hunger.

Someone wearing white led me into a little room and told me to wait there for the doctor. Some several minutes later he arrived. He took one look at me and said, "I'll be back in a minute." When he came back he had a photocopied handout in his hand. He launched into a discussion of my weight. I interrupted him (I see doctors as large human pez dispensers who hand out drugs when necessary, I experience no awe in their presence) and told him that the problem was not my weight but that I had a throat infection which may have spread to my ear.

He nodded knowingly and stated that I was far above my ideal body weight and should probably take a look at his handout at a weight loss diet. I took the diet out of politeness and a feeling that I could get him to talk about my throat if I humoured him. I thanked him for his concern and then talked about my throat. He barely nodded and then began to tell me the dangers about being significantly overweight. "My THROAT AND EAR!" I was beyond politeness.

He got a flashlight and begrudgingly approached me. The position he needed to stand in to get close enough to look down my largest orifice put my knee in an interesting position. I had a delightful image that is quite unprofessional but I realized that a single sharp gesture would irrevocably change both of our histories. Me, I'd be in jail for assault (but if I was lucky and there was even one fat person on the jury I would end up with a jury hung better than the doctor probably was!) Him, he'd end up singing falsetto in a drag band. He informed me with some surprise that I had a throat infection. Checking my ear, he noted that it had spread to my ear. I would need antibiotics. (They go to school for this?) Yes, indeed. After getting the prescription, I gave him back the diet and told him where he could put it. He got angry and told me that I was being offensive.

I told him that until boiling those pieces of paper could cure a sore throat and an ear ache they should stay in his desk where they belonged. True, I am fat but the solution to every medical problem is not "lose weight." We had some harsh words that would best be left unwritten. I would like to tell you that I said something cute and funny but I was sick and angry. I didn't have the energy for much beyond good old faithful obscenities although I like to think I combined them in an interesting fashion.

The idea that since I am fat there is only one solution to every medical problem I have is fraught with the same kind of bigotry that believing that behaviour approaches are the only solution to every maladaptive behaviour shown by a person with a disability. Part of the job of people who support people with disabilities is asking the right questions. I shudder to think what would have happened if I had been a person with a disability who was accompanied by a staff who was shy about speaking up to doctors. There is no question in my mind that my throat and ear would have been ignored and I would have been put on a diet.

There are a number of non-behaviour hypotheses that you need to investigate as part of your decision about what to do regarding peoples' behaviour. The treatment for each of these is out of your hands but it is up to you to ask the right questions and be persistent in your demands of other professionals.

Medical

The referral was typical. It was for aggression and acting out behaviour for a young man with a developmental disability who worked in a sheltered industry. On investigation with the front line staff it was clear that they had become quite frightened of him and explained that he would go right out of control. When asking if anyone had been seriously hurt by him, they stated that one person had been cut by falling glass. Apparently when he was very upset he would throw things at the ceiling and often would break the fluorescent tubing and it would shower down on the workers. After some discussion it became clear that he did show some control. He never purposefully hurt another person, he would damage the environment and as a side effect someone might get hurt.

The staff felt that there was no clear reason for the

behaviour but that they noticed an odd pattern. It seemed that he would be more likely to have an outburst during the beginning of the week rather than the end of the week. In fact, when checking the incident reports, it became clear that this was entirely a Monday-Tuesday behaviour. It wasn't every Monday and Tuesday so it wasn't clear what might be setting him off. Observations were set up and it didn't take long to realize that there was very little variety in a day. In fact, if one didn't look at the calendar one would not have been able to tell one day from the next. Contracts came in, contracts were done, contracts were sent out. Clearly there was no particular provocation for the behaviour during early parts of the week.

This caused a quandry. We know that whenever there is a clear pattern of behaviour there is an antecedent. We could find none. Thinking about this with my university educated brain, I thought to myself, "Gee, Mondays and Tuesdays feel differently to me than do Thursdays and Fridays because of the presence of the weekend." No fool me!!! We then thought that a meeting needed to be called with residential services. They might be able to tell us what had happened on the weekends where there had been outbursts. This seems reasonable, logical even, but we know that in human services this is dangerous. Getting residential services and vocational services into a room is much like getting warring states to agree to a mutual peace. With some work they both agreed to the meeting.

Once together and focussed on the problem we pulled out the data from the sheltered industry. The residential service worker stated that the last outburst was immediately after Daniel had made a visit to his parents. We all nodded knowingly, parents are a problem you see, and looked to see if there were other possible causes. After reviewing all the dates and looking at his visits to his parents it was clear that 100% of the problems occurred when he was out of our control and in his parents' home. Well, did we have a good time with that one. Human service workers are notorious parent haters. We kind of figure we could have done better than them on all counts, except of course in the little matter of love. A scheduled visit was coming up and we predicted that he would have an outburst when he returned to work the next Monday. And guess what? We were right!

We felt then that Daniel was using his behaviours to tell us that he was not happy at home, that he wanted to terminate his visits. We began to wonder what was happening in his home. Was there abuse? What did those evil people do to him anyways? We scheduled a meeting with the executive director to discuss the possibility of terminating his home visits. Clearly his behaviour was communicating that there was a problem. We noted that when they visited him in his home there was no outburst, it was only when he was *WITH THEM* that the problem occurred. The executive director felt that maybe we needed to get other authorization for our plan. He suggested that we go to the doctor and get the doctor to make the recommendation to terminate visits. That way the parents would be angry at the doctor and not us. GOOD PLAN .... transfer responsibility and cover the butt!!!!

At the doctor's office we presented the data. The

doctor agreed that there was a clear correlation but then asked what we had seen on our visit to the family home. I was insulted. I am a behaviourist, I can read data, I can count, I can develop hypotheses, I can forget the obvious. This seemed logical. A visit was arranged wherein Daniel, his primary staff from the residence and myself would visit him in his home with his parents. Just a lunch on a Sunday, mind you. When we got there what did we find. A lovely elderly couple. Now this was a shock, I had built these people up in my mind to be Jeffery Dalhmer and Tanya Harding, only older and meaner. We had a lovely lunch.

Now, do you think I was going to change my hypothesis just because what I saw didn't match what I predicted. NOT ON YOUR LIFE. I simply said to myself, "Abusers can be kindly little old ladies bearing plates of date squares. I can't be fooled!" When we left I said to the front line staff that since we were there we changed the interactions and therefore there would not be an outburst the following Monday.

Monday there was a doozy.

Now, do you think I was going to change my hypothesis just because I couldn't use it to predict behaviour? NOT ON YOUR LIFE. I said to myself, "Well just *BEING IN A THAT HOUSE WITH THOSE TWO OLD PEOPLE IS ENOUGH TO CAUSE HIM SIGNIFICANT DISTRESS.*" Back to the doctor we went. We presented our findings to him. He could not believe that we didn't see any thing between parents and child that would cause this kind of extreme reaction in Daniel.

We assured him that Daniel was never out of our sight and that they were very nice to him. We talked about lunch and chattered about the home. A light turned on in the doctor's eyes and he reached for another file. It contained the consultations he had done with the agency.

He found in the file a notation that at one point about three months previous, around the time the outbursts started, he had done a consultation to the then group home manager. Group home workers are kind of like pages in a dirty book -- turnover is high, fast, often dramatic and the residue can be quite sticky. The group home manager had come to the doctor to discuss diet. She felt that the diet in the group home was way too high in sugar and way too low in fibre. She wondered if he could recommend a healthier diet. This he did. They had adopted his recommended dietary change in the group home. He then asked us, "What did they feed Daniel on his visit?" Well, they fed him his favourite foods, I hadn't particularly noticed because they were my favourite foods too, delicious, high in sugar, low in nutrients, MMMM MMMMM MMMMM. He then scheduled a test for Daniel and it was discovered that he had hypoglycaemia which has been linked to outburst behaviour.

We were asked to contact the parents and tell them that Daniel needed to eat less sugar and that his pattern of eating would have to change. They immediately agreed to make the change because, of course, they loved their son. Daniel's outbursts stopped.

This example scares me. Look at what we had done. We had done observations, read data, made predictions and built an excellent hypothesis. Don't get me wrong the hypothesis was excellent and founded on a good reading of the data, the only problem with it was that it was wrong. Look also at what we were going to do to Daniel, for his own good. We were going to tear him out of his home, thereby destroying the only ongoing relationship he had in his life. And guess what!!! We would never have found our error. Why? Because his behaviour would have changed, but because of the diet in the home, not because of his family relationship.

The medical hypothesis is incredibly important, so much so that it should be a rule that no behaviour is investigated without a medical being done. The trouble with the medical hypothesis is that many conditions and illnesses are invisible and if the client can't communicate them they will have to use their behaviour to communicate.

****

I'M GETTING ON MY HIGH HORSE NOW

Even when the illness is quite visible, it doesn't mean that we are any more likely to be compassionate. How many times have you seen a person with a developmental disability who is very sick being sent to work in the morning anyways just because it is too expensive for them to stay home? We, on the other hand get to take days off because of stress. I guess people with disabilities don't FEEL a cold the way we do. I guess people with disabilities don't FEEL stress like we do. What other way can you explain the difference in how we pamper ourselves and how we impatiently push people with disabilities out the door, with hankies, nose drops, a vitamin and a see you later?

I'M GETTING OFF MY HIGH HORSE NOW
(usually having made an ass of myself!)

****

Medications and Their Side Effects

It was a referral I'll never forget. There it was right on the referral sheet right after the question NATURE OF PROBLEM BEHAVIOUR: Penis slapping against the wall behaviour. Now when I read this I have to admit that I was angry at the fact that he could slap his penis against the wall. Me? I would have to run hard *AT* the wall. Nonetheless, the penis slapping against the wall was upsetting other residents and staff. What .... did the noise keep them up? Did he dent the wall? Do I really get paid to do this?

When meeting with the staff we all managed to

keep a straight face. Well, actually all the guys tried to look professional and the women kept smirking. Nonetheless we bravely carried on and I asked when the behaviour began. I was told that it had begun around Christmas time. Now what on earth does penis slapping against the wall behaviour have to do with Christmas time except that it's another way to Deck the Halls? "Did anything special happen at Christmas?" I asked, and was told that he made a parent visit. (There are those damn parents again.) Well, I had actually learned from Daniel and didn't make any assumptions. How had his Christmas visit gone? They assumed that it went well but weren't sure. I called the family to see how Christmas went and if the visit was a good one. Now, I have to tell you I think that most of these kinds of calls to parents are very cruel. No way was I going to pick up the phone and call perfect strangers to say, "Hi, my name is Dave and your son is slapping his penis against the wall. Oh, and by the by how was Christmas?" I mean really, all I needed to know was how the visit had gone. They told me that Christmas had been better than they expected. It was wonderful.

I asked the staff why they might have anticipated a bad visit and they told me that the client was a behaviour problem and was on a number of behaviour programmes. The parents were nice but not great programmers, everyone anticipated the worst. I began to go through the file and looked at meeting minutes. These are the most interesting thing in a file. The incident reports are basically just therapeutic outlets for staff anger, the data is mostly made up just before a behaviour therapist arrives and the reports home are mostly Hallmark hollow. Ah, but meeting minutes where we document what we do, that's interesting. There I found an interesting meeting that happened in the early part of November where they were discussing his upcoming visit home. They were worried that when he was away from programming consistency that he might have serious outbursts. They decided that they should increase his medications for the time he was at home. Sure enough the meds were increased but I could find no evidence that they were ever returned to their original level once he returned home. This gave the team an idea and we looked up in the medication books and discovered that he was on a medication that affected penile functioning. Clearly this young man was dealing with the frustration that came from having his penis simply stop working, without explanation and without understanding he was trying to increase the stimulation to his penis.

WHAT YOU CAN DO

✔Medication side effects are extremely important yet often doctors forget (?) to tell us that the drugs we are taking will cure stiff necks but cause limp glans. Therefore it's up to you. No you aren't a medical doctor but you are an advocate. First and easiest ASK THE DOCTOR about side effects. Remember that medications taken singly have certain side effects and medications taken in combinations have a different set of side effects. So ASK. I'm putting this in capital letters because I can't reach through the pages and howl the words at you. I know that doctors treat front line staff as if you are just barely out of evolutionary sludge but don't let them intimidate you. It's your job to be assertive and to ensure that your client is getting good service. Second, go and buy a reference book that lists medications and their side effects. Check and make sure that the doctor has given you all the information you need. Remember lots of doctors were in the bottom third of their class.

Psychiatric

The idea that people with developmental disabilities have an internal emotive structure still is controversial. Many assume or openly state that people with disabilities don't have the same capacity to feel, physically or emotionally, as non disabled people. In fact, I believe that it was this assumption more than any other that lead to institutionalization in the first place. If they don't feel physical pain in the same way as you or I, then why not use extreme measures like electric shock? If they don't feel emotional pain, why not pull them out of their parents' homes and put them into human warehouses?

Not long ago I sat at my friends' Bruce and Shirl's place eating donuts and drinking tea. Their daughter dropped by and told of her first experience working in an institution for people with disabilities. She said that they literally shovelled food into troughs and used hoses to wash people down. These same people have come out of institutions and into the community. Is it any wonder that many have emotional scars?

The first person I met who had a disability and was receiving psychiatric service was John. I had known him for maybe two days. Starting a new job and getting my bearings was stressful and exciting. John was one of several men who were placed under my control because I had done well in an interview.

I faced a large interview team that asked few questions about who I was, preferring to concentrate on what I had done. The answer to the latter question was, "Very little." Even so, I must have impressed them somewhat because they gave me the job. Actually, the phone was ringing when I walked into my apartment. A start date was set, and I celebrated.

Walking onto the ward was frightening. This was the ward for the behaviour problems. They were kept behind a locked door and unbreakable glass. Staff had a room, the nursing office, that was set inside the ward but accessible only from the hallway. From that room one could see the two main rooms, the day room and the television room. The only thing that made these rooms separate was that the day room had a few dining tables and the television room had a television.

Someone had painted pictures from Snow White and the Seven Dwarfs on the walls. They were bright and colourful pictures that were unnoticed by the staff or the men who lived there. In the corner of the day room was a locked door that lead to a small kitchen. The bedroom door was just barely visible from the nursing office.

John lived here. He was a tall lanky man whose prize possession was a wallet made bulky with hundreds of photographs. He paced back and forth. I noticed him from the first day when I sat and read files in the nursing office. His pacing had the sense of ritual. He had a reputation for violence, although I never saw him out of control. He paced the ward, sleeping little and constantly mumbling under his breath. His bulky wallet had been stuffed with hundreds of pictures from magazines. Every now and then he would sit down, this was rare for him because he always moved, rocking even as he walked. When he sat he would pull out the wallet at look at the pictures and talk to them. They had become his family and he would plead for them to come and take him home. They never came.

One day I was asked to escort him to the psychiatric hospital for ECT. I was new to the job. I was new to the field. I had learned about this procedure in the classroom just months before. Somehow sitting in the classroom discussing this procedure, it was all academic, it was all so sterile, it was just an abstraction. What it wasn't was a strong electric current that ran through someone's brain as punishment for some past acting out that left him with a current label. What it wasn't was a man who shuffled about fighting for memory and fighting for a sense of self and a sense of permanence. What it wasn't was a man who spent his days walking trying to escape another trip to the table where his brain was violated. What it wasn't was a man who had lost family, been caged and who looked at kind faces cut out of magazines for hope of his escape.

My next contact with someone who was dually diagnosed was working with a woman with a disability who hid under a bed and witnessed the murder of her parents. She moved to a group home and spent her time alternating between a general states of anxiety and bouts of pure fear. She started every time someone came to the door. She cried whenever she heard sounds that reminded her of her parents' screams. She could not cope with television news programs or any show that involved murder. Take out violence and there are practically no television shows left. The staff and other residents were understanding for awhile. A very brief while. Then it was time for medication. She clearly was paranoid. She clearly had lost grasp of reality. She clearly needed medications to cope with her fear.

Now I understood that medications were important and discussing them we can be practical, we can be dispassionate, we can maintain professional distance. That's because medications are a therapeutic approach which is simply practical. What it isn't is a woman who fought taking the medication because she saw them as taking away her ability to protect herself. What it isn't is a woman who crawled under her bed at night to sleep because this was the only place safe from violence. What is isn't is a woman whose feelings have been taken from her. For her own good, of course.

All this left me, and many in the field of developmental disability, very sceptical of the whole idea of psychiatric approaches to developmental handicap. Then I heard Dr. Robert Sovner speak for the first time. He talked about how important it was to understand the emotive and physical worlds of people with developmental disabilities. We talked afterwards and he did a consultation for us regarding a man who heard voices that were transmitted through radio waves to televisions and radios. These voices called him names, told him he was "Retarded" and "Stupid." These voices tormented him through his nights and he had begun hitting his ears, punishing them for allowing the sounds in.

When we first talked with Dr. Sovner, this man had been placed in a psychiatric ward and we were desperate. Behaviour approaches were out of the question. Unless we could find a way to program the voices we were in trouble. Dr. Sovner took a lot of time with us, diagnosed a problem and gave this man some medication ... that's not fair, what he gave this man was relief and control. Sure it came in a pill but that's what it was. He then suggested that we needed to pursue his fears and work to establish a place where he feels safe. He suggested that some work on his self concept and inner language was necessary. So this is what ethical psychiatric treatment of a person with a disability looks like.

It became clear to me that to leave out of the analysis possible psychiatric illness was unfair and biased. True it has been misused with folks with developmental disabilities, but so has behaviour therapy, community living and integration. Dr. Sovner taught me that a technique or approach is never responsible for those who use it. As I began working with people with disabilities who had been victimized, Dr. Ruth Ryan came as answer to prayer and talked about post traumatic stress syndrome with people with developmental disability. She encourages people to understand that some people with disabilities have lived in pure hell, even with torture. Then there was Sue Gabriel, a down to earth, practical and kind Psychiatric Nurse Practitioner. My attitude changed. In the light of kindness and compassion.

A newsletter created by and for people with diabilities, called MOUTH, described situations in a treatment facility that had walls decorated with child-like characters even though the treatment was for adults. The author described the facility as "Auschwitz on Sesame Street." Given that this is the viewpoint of people who have been there, can it be anything but pertinent to hear Dr. Ryan's plea for us to understand that we work often with survivors, no we work with ... SURVIVORS!!

These psychiatrists have integrated into their work an understanding of disability, an evaluation of the places those with disabilities live and expertise in illness of the human mind and the human heart. They demonstrate that it is necessary to understand people with developmental disabilities as fully human and therefore complex psychological creatures who just may be dealing with trauma, victimization, a sense of loss or any of a thousand psychological issues. (A psychiatrist friend of mine told me that an ace psychiatrist has to be an expert in "faces, spaces and places.")

WHAT YOU CAN DO

✔Inform yourself. This is a flat out endorsement. The Habilitative Mental Healthcare Newsletter is a "must" subscription. This newsletter is put out every two months and has clearly written articles that outline psychiatric supports for people with developmental disabilities. This resource is invaluable in giving suggestions for service. Too, by the very nature of the articles one realizes the breadth of services needed by people with disabilities. Our office has given copies of this journal as seasonal presents for psychiatrists in the area that we work. This way it supports the work of the journal as well as gets the information into the hands of professionals who serve our clients.

✔Get support. There is an organization called the National Association for the Dually Diagnosed that has an annual conference. This conference is a place where professionals can meet with others who face dealing with people who are coping with emotional illness while having a developmental disability. I found that this organization enabled me to meet many incredible people who see people with disabilities as being complex and as having the capacity to feel and heal. They produce their own newsletter and have created a means of people who work in the field of developmental disability and mental illness to meet one another and develop a common language.

Significant Life Change

"Refusing to eat!" I know that my voice showed shock. As a large person I have a wonderful relationship with food. I love it and it loves me right back. So much so that the lollipops I gorged on as a child are still stored in little fat cells somewhere under what is supposed to be my waist. Isn't it great to love something that will stay with you forever! Through thin and thick! So the idea that someone would voluntarily refuse food when it was offered was past my comprehension. I asked if he refused all food at all times. I was told that he hadn't eaten for days and that in the last day or so he had begun to refuse all liquid as well. The doctor had pronounced him as fit and had no idea as to why his appetite had just died. A recommendation had been made to offer him a variety of foods until he chose something. They then told me that they had a garbage pail full of McDonald's hamburgers and a variety of take out pizzas were stored in the fridge untouched. This goes beyond serious this is sick! I thought it best to get up there and interview him and see about that pizza in the fridge. Couldn't be too careful you know.

Clearly we were worried. What might be causing this? We drove up to the institution where the man lived and commented on how quiet the building was now that it was empty. This man was about to make the move to a new community and a new home from a smallish institution. His placement wasn't ready so he and the five that would move with him had moved into smaller quarters behind the main building which had been closed. The place was pleasant enough and the other men seemed quite happy to be out of the big building and were looking forward to the move. But not Ted. Ted was listless, bored and completely uninterested in any activities. I sat with him and offered him a coffee, he pushed it away. He wasn't rude he was just uninterested. There wasn't much conversation either. Ted couldn't talk much and seemed to find just being with me an effort.

I went to the file. There was nothing here to tell me why he was acting the way he was. Too, I was confused. I had seen some depression amongst the men who had moved from this facility to their new homes. The transition was hard for some of them and it was work to get them settled. But this man wasn't in transition yet.

He was still on the grounds of the only home he had known for twenty years, this shouldn't be happening. The file proved useless. I turned to the staff, none could give me any information. All of them were new to Ted. The people who had cared for Ted all those years in the institution were long gone. No one knew anything and Ted wouldn't or couldn't talk. We were stymied. Days went by as more food was offered, more was turned down. He refused to take an anti-depressant and sought more and more time alone, away from the others who grew boisterous at the idea of moving to their new home.

There had been a name in the file that had appeared over and over again. A woman had signed most of the reports and had documented most of the concerns over the last ten years of Ted's life. Maybe we could find her. The idea was approved, the call was made and the appointment set. We met an angry woman, she had seen deinstitutionalization as a condemnation of her life's work. She had tried to support and provide a secure atmosphere for those on her ward and she felt slapped by the normalization movement. She didn't trust us or our motives. It was a tense beginning. When we told her about what was happening with Ted, tears filled her eyes. She said that she wasn't surprised that he was reacting this way, she was surprised it was so severe, but she wasn't surprised. We asked her to share the information with us.

She refused!

Out and out refused! She said that she felt the information was confidential and she felt that it was the kind of thing that could damage Ted and his reputation.

She felt that we might use the information to hurt him not help him. She felt that neither he, nor she, could trust us. We begged her. She finally agreed to tell us only on the condition that she be informed and consulted all along the way regarding work with Ted. We agreed.

Then we were told. Ted had been in love with another man on the ward of the institution. They had carried on a relationship for at least ten years. She said that they had been lovers when she arrived and she had been there for ten years. We were then told that the staff had decided that what was going on was no one's business. They spent lots of time together on the ward and would help each other with grooming and dressing. They would sit close together and seemed to understand each other. Staff didn't know exactly where they had sex but were sure that they did. In truth, she said, they felt that it was best just to leave them alone.

She thought that the problem was that no one had explained that deinstitutionalization meant that each man would be sent to a different part of the province. Ted woke up one morning and found that the man he had loved well and steadily for ten years was gone. She felt that he was probably mourning the loss of his lover. He needed, she felt, to know that the man he loved was still alive.

We called a meeting and brought this forward. The issue made everyone uncomfortable. We had to talk about what this man had lost and how the change brought about by deinstitutionalization had taken from him the best and most important part of his life. We had to talk about what to do and how to do it. In the best of all possible worlds these two men would have been reunited. But no, this is not the best of all possible worlds, the men were brought back in touch with each other and visits were set up.

I was not there the day they saw each other again, but I'm told they had lunch.

Deinsititutionalization brings a number of significant changes. A person loses home, friends, social atmosphere, job, purpose, routine and a million other things. True, they get these back and the quality of life offered in the community can be so much greater that the transition period is worth the effort. But change causes stress. People with disabilities are not immune to stress and in fact have even more than most of us because they have little control or input into the changes in their lives.

Significant life changes can be as great as deinstitutionalization and as small as a staff change. When evaluating why someone has started to act up or have a change in temperament, look critically at their life. Write down all the changes that have occurred in the months preceding the "acting up." What has gone on? Who has left? What changed at work?

Don't dismiss anything. We may not think that it's significant that John and Mary no longer sit at the same worktable at the sheltered industry. They never talked anyways. Why would that make a difference? Well John and Mary may have communicated to each other in a thousand ways that are almost invisible to the naked eye.

They may miss each other. So, WRITE IT DOWN. Then take a look at the list if it is long with a bunch of little changes, or if it's short with one big change, you may have found the source of the problem.

WHAT YOU CAN DO

✔Cope Just Cope: Once a person's life has been disrupted by events, within or out of personal control it is impossible to return to a previous state of calm. You are just going to have to ride through the transition period as the client settles into a new routine or a new realization. You may want to write a behaviour program but this probably isn't necessary. If the hypothesis of Significant Life Change is the cause of the behaviour then view the problem as a momentary blip in the person's life span. True it seems like forever because you have to work through it with them. But trust me, once stability returns then the person will be back to normal. Give them time.

Hey, don't you need people to be just a little more patient with YOU when you are going through trying times? Have you ever bitten someone's head off and then apologized later? Did you say something like, "Sorry, I had to deal with my child being home sick and I can't be there. I was just plain mad this morning." After the explanation what do you expect? Probably nothing more than understanding. When a person is going through a significant life change then what they need is time and understanding.

✔Cope Just Cope: While the points are labelled the same, this one is intended for the people you serve.

Very few people with disabilities have been taught any coping strategies. When there is a problem they may simply act or react to the stress by just exploding. Here's where you probably feel quite superior because you would never react with violence, destruction or self injury. Bull! You do, and you do quite regularly. But you do it in your head. When you are upset what do you do to calm yourself down? Do you sit quietly and picture yourself in a quiet meadow with larks flying by singing songs that tinkle into the distance? Do you picture wind blowing gently over the meadow and the heads of the long grass just swinging and swaying in the breeze? Do you picture yourself walking into the babbling brook and feel the cool of the water wash over your bare feet? Do you picture holding your boss' head in the water and keeping it there while he struggles? Now you lift it up, now push it back under, now up, now under. You lift your head back and laugh maniacally as you see his eyes bulge under the water. Yes! Yes!!! Oooops. You can guess what kind of day I've had.

The point being you act out all the time but you just do it in your head and can easily let off steam this way. Well, many people with disabilities do the same thing only they act out what we think. Our thinking and violent visualization is a coping skill. We would never do, or say, many of the things that come to our mind but we have the impulses. We need to teach people with disabilities to deal with the same impulses we have. While it may be unrealistic, and unwise, to teach people with disabilities to imagine all sorts of violent acts they could do to the staff, there are numerous other coping skills. Learning to recognize their upset and escape the situation before they lose control. Learning to set oneself apart when one needs privacy. Learning to express pain, disappointment in words or through emotions. These are all skills and people need to learn them. Life is a series of changes and most of them we can't control. We have to learn to cope.

Past learning personal coping skills, remember that if you are in a situation that is personally demanding you may want to talk to a counsellor about it. This option is very seldom explored for people with disabilities. I believe and have seen that regular counselling has helped a person learn to express their feelings and to have an outlet where they can, in a safe environment, talk about what they are dealing with. Don't forget that if a person has lost a parent, lost a home or been abused they may just need professional help in learning to cope with the loss or the hurt.

✔Create Security: Inasmuch as people with disabilities live in systems where they are often seen as pawns in the game of residential placements, we can do a lot of things to build a system that sees people living in homes not houses and that people with disabilities are, well, people, not beds. It is important that any agency which would provide residential services has several meetings and recognize that if they are going to provide QUALITY care then they must see stability as a major attribute of the system. Many agencies will move clients almost as an intellectual exercise.

"Gee, we can put Bill in this house and that would free up the space over here. Since the two guys who live there are near sixty we can move Sam from here and Ashley from there both into the house and this will create a home where we can staff for people who are elderly. Now if Ashley and Sam are going to move what about the spaces in their house? As to staffing, Helen has said that she isn't interested in working in a home for elderly people so let's move her with Bill and the staff from Ashley's home has quit so let's move the others and distribute so that we have some staff who are experienced in each of the homes."

ISN'T THIS FUN? No. Not if you are any of the people being discussed. Their life is about to go into turmoil and when they react they will be seen as a behaviour problem rather than a person under a great deal of stress. Does this make sense? A book like this can't give concrete advice about how to handle this problem because every agency is different, but it is possible to suggest that you have to discuss this to ensure that stability and security are high on the list of descriptors of your group homes and living situations.

✔Prepare For Changes: Even in agencies that are careful to provide stable living environments, some changes are necessary. Some clients will want to move to new places. Some will want to change jobs. Some will want to try new experiences that will require they move or that there is a staff change. These things happen. (You will note that these are all changes that the client wants and is looking forward to.) Even with these kinds of changes they bring with them stress. Don't they for you? There is an approach that we have used that has really helped with this process.

A brilliant man named Dr. Peter Dowrick uses a procedure called "self modelling." In this procedure he uses a video camera to make a self model film to teach skills. We have used this procedure many times with great effectiveness. One situation where I have used this procedure is when a person is facing a major change in their life, such as leaving an institution or going to work in a new environment. Knowing that I prepare for personal change by thinking and imagining myself in my own future, I wondered about people with disabilities. Are they able to prepare themselves in the same way?

Think about when you last moved, did you imagine yourself in your new home, walking through your new neighbourhood, cooking in your new kitchen? If you did you were using a "film" made in your head to prepare yourself for the change. Adapting Dr. Dowrick's procedure here is simple. We take someone to a new environment a few weeks before the change and then make a film of them living, working or coping in the new environment. When they come home we simply let them watch themselves in their future once or twice a day. The films aren't elaborate but they are enough to let the person prepare for a change in the same way you and I do.

Life Space Analysis

And then there was Mary Ann. Nothing worked with Mary Ann, or worked for very long with her. She was a behaviourist's nightmare. No matter what hypothesis, no matter how well planned the contingencies or how consistent the staff, she would frustrate the program and the staff. Staff had become leary of any program success because, at first it would seem to work and then....

An explosion would occur and she she would have a temper tantrum that would leave all of us in AWE. She musta burned some 16 million calories in the space of 4 or 5 SECONDS. This was a woman who made temper tantrumming an Olympic sport. She did everything but spin her head around and spit out pea soup. She was SCARY.

I looked at her environment, a pleasantly appointed group home with other people with disabilities at a similar state in their personal growth. (How's that for avoiding arrest by the politically correct police?!) When she moved in, the place and her seemed to agree. Then, just as we thought all those reports from the institution were gross exaggeration, she threw a doozy. Pulling kitchen chairs out of the walls and moving the refrigerator off the lawn, we realized that Mary Ann had a bit of a problem with temper control. Trying to use procedures like deep breathing relaxation with someone who has a hammer lock on your scrotum seemed a little naive, so we attempted other temper control techniques.

Not much worked, we discovered a new form of art as Mary Ann would take her M & M reinforcers and schmuck them against the wallpaper in a mud made of spit and snot. Given modern art we could have sold them for a fortune. Other reinforcers were equally unsuccessful, particularly the tokens. What she did with the tokens is legendary and modesty forbids me from being so graphic. We were in crisis, Mary Ann was in control. Then a discovery, by chance. One of the staff, terrified, asked Mary Ann if she wanted to go for a drive. This does not seem brave but when windows are broken and staff and clients are cowering in a corner a little outing seems a bit dangerous. Mary Ann quickly agreed and out they went. Once in the car she seemed to really settle down quickly.

The staff questioned her and it seemed that Mary Ann really wanted to get out of the house. The drive seemed to settle her down. When we next met about her we thought that maybe being stuck in a house, even one that is tastefully appointed, was driving her to distraction. We then thought about this issue, what if we each had to spend all of our time in a place that we loved, with people that we loved. What if we never got to leave their presence. Would it drive us to distraction? It would. We then talked about "honeymooning." Isn't it possible that a person does well in a new environment until they feel stuck with no way out? Isn't it possible that people learn tantrums as a way to gain privacy, to gain control, to get out of somewhere?

This kind of questioning is looking at life space analysis. What we are doing is looking critically at the place the person lives, how they fit into that place and how they can utilize their skills to make it in that place. It has always disturbed me to see people talk about privacy as a sexual issue when it is actually a mental health issue. I couldn't make it through my job without a few moments that I could just shut down and close out all the stressors. Thankfully, I have a secretary that can screen calls and at home I can stand over my answering machine and say nasty things to callers I don't want to talk to. Not that I would, but I could.

WHAT YOU CAN DO

✔Examine the Peg. Examine the Hole. While we have all heard about trying to stick square pegs into round holes, few have ever really understood this issue. Seeing people with disabilities who hate noise, small places and repetitive work having to cope with noise, small places and repetitive work because the sheltered industry is noisy, small and does repetitive contract work is so commonplace that it seems ridiculous. Even so when in meetings and discussing that people hate their jobs, their homes, their roommates and then hearing that the solution is to make them calm down and cope with hating their homes, their jobs and their roommates is absurd. In a country where people can't seem to stay married for more than 5 to 10 minutes it's a bit hypocritical to suggest that people with disabilities are "behaviour problems" for trying to get out of situations that we would just leave.

This is not an easy thing. It involves learning the likes and dislikes of a person and then seeing how their personal idiosyncracies fit with their environments. The reason that this is not easy is because it requires getting to know a person and seeing how they react to a variety of situations and a variety of settings. Their behaviour will speak volumes when their words cannot. Don't be fooled by those interviews that we do with people. I have seen any number of new forms and questions asked of a person regarding their likes and wants. These questions are fine for people who have learned to speak for themselves and further have learned their own likes and dislikes because they have lived and experimented. But for a person with a disability to have to answer the question, "Do you like your home?" when asked by a staff in that home, when asked without ever having seen other ways of living, when asked without understanding there isn't a "right" answer other than their own opinion is unfair. Get to know the peg and then you can tell if the hole is too big, too small or too confining.

✔Ensure Breaks and Build in Privacy: Even when a person loves the place and likes the people, make sure they have opportunities to get out of those places and have moments every day where they can be alone. Don't go forcing them into rooms for privacy but just make sure that they can have it when they want. Too, learn to read a person's behaviour and teach them to ask for escape. It's better for them to say that they would like to go away for a weekend than to perform behaviours that have us sending them away for a lifetime.

Interactional Support

It's a moment I won't soon forget. The day had been a typical one when I'm on the road lecturing. I began with a consultation in the morning, moved on to lunch and then was beginning an afternoon presentation to be followed by dinner and then the evening presentation. A long day, but I like my work and when I'm on the road sometimes work is preferable to sitting alone in a hotel room. I had just begun the lecture and something went wrong. My heart started to pound in my chest and the world started to go blurry. I thought that I was going to die. Now, I don't know about you but I don't want to die in front of an audience so I said to the audience "I think I am going to die," and left the room heading outside into the fresh air. While I tried to reattach myself to the ground I knew that there was an audience full of people thinking, "Gee, I wonder if the fat guy is going to die." Too, the organizers would be thinking, "Do we have to give the money back?"

Once I had gotten air back into my body I went back in and finished the lecture. I held on to the podium for support and gave the lecture purely by rote. After it was done one of the organizers wanted to know what we should do about the evening presentation. "What!?" How am I supposed to make that kind of decision while I am in crisis. I suggested we simply go back to the hotel room. When we got there she asked again what should be done about the evening. I told her to just come back and get me and we would make decisions then, I had to get into my room and lie down.

I will not kid you here, I was terrified. I am a fat man and I know all about weight and heart attacks (although I must insert here that it annoys me that when  a thin man my age has a heart attack it is a tragedy and when a fat man has a heart attack, he deserves it). Now when I got back into my room do you think I sat down and simply problem solved? Absolutely not, *I WAS IN A CRISIS, I DON'T THINK WELL IN A CRISIS.*

I called home and engaged in whining behaviour. I explained quickly and breathlessly that I in trouble and I was scared. I got just what was needed, a firm but calming voice asked me to state my symptoms exactly without "Hingsburger hyperbole" and I did as I was told. I was asked what I had had for lunch. The question took me by surprise but I answered that we had gone to a seafood place and that I had had crab salad. Then I was told to get off the phone and call the restaurant. When I asked why, I was told that my symptoms seemed to be an extreme reaction to MSG. I have always had a sensitivity to MSG and would often complain about shortness of breath and slight dizziness after dinners out. Maybe, I was told, it was worse because I was in a charged state because of lecturing. I hung up and called the restaurant and was told that the food was loaded with MSG.

I called home. I was then told to lie down. "Dave, you take a nap. Don't worry about the wake up call. I'll do the wake up call. You just sleep. Oh, and Dave I know you think that this needs to be worried about, so I'll do the worrying the worrying will get done. You just sleep."

I got the wake up call and made it through the evening presentation and through the rest of the trip.

Please note that I did not make it through the evening because I could stand up. I made it through the evening because I was held up. When in crisis I lost control of my emotions, fear overcame me. When I lost control of my emotions, I lost all decision making skills. When I lost all decision making skills, I had to rely on someone I trusted to get me through the situation. Luckily I have someone who can do that for me.

From this I realized that I make it through my life, my job and my relationships, personal and professional, because I have an incredible support network. There are people out there who can step in and give me what I need when I need it. These are the people who know when they have to take control and when I am ready to take it back.

WHAT YOU CAN DO

✔Sensitize Yourself. Ask yourself how many times you make it through your day because someone voluntarily helps you. How many times when you have wanted to plow your boss right in the kisser a co-worker has given you the time and space to let out the steam? How many times when you felt unwanted and unappreciated at work have you walked down the hall and had a friend give you a thumbs up or a little wink that completely changed your day? More than this how many times have you been saved from doing tissue damage to your child because you could pick up the phone and let a stream of forbidden words run along the wire into someone else's understanding? Who are these people to you? At a staff meeting have a number of people jot down their support network. Who are these people? You will find that the support network varies but is quite similar. Family, friends, co-workers, ministers, some will put God on the list as someone to talk to in times of trouble. Your support network is probably fairly deep.

Now take a look at your clients. Who is in their network? If it is limited, then you may have found the source of many problems. No human being, I believe, has all the functional coping skills to live life in relation to others without help. We all are prevented from crimes as serious as murder because we have people who help us deal with VERY REAL angers, anxieties and animosities. These feelings are strong and we need more than our "self control" to deal with them. Help build this network.

✔Examine Expectations and Roles. Two things come to mind here. First, I have seen staff take people with disabilities who are in crisis, through temper or fear, and ask them to talk about it. That's smart. Firstly, when I'm angry I can't rationally talk about anything. I want to let it out, I want to scream and say things that are so socially inappropriate that they would be considered serious enough to record on an incident report and be placed into my file. Secondly, when people are angry or sad they often can't explain why right then. Have you ever been depressed and had someone ask you why you were sad? Could you answer the question? The expectation that a person with a disability can do things when upset that no one else can is bizarre.

What we want at this time is not a rational discussion, nor is it advice. We need someone to give us time and space and we need someone to take some of the control we lost. We allow this only because we trust that they will give it back to us. Unfortunately, if staff are the sole form of support for someone, we need to work with them towards the day that they don't need to rely just on people paid to be there.

✔Respect Support Networks. Whenever I hear people talk at meetings about people with disabilities and we move to the subject of support networks, invariably we talk about developing appropriate friendships. What this always means is non-disabled people in relationship to people with disabilities. A real friend, as determined by the philosophically sure and the politically correct, is a person without a disability. In fact, when someone has a friend with a disability this is sometimes seen as a problem. Moreover should they want to go out together as a group of friends people go crazy! This can't happen. No, stop!

This gets to the point of absurdity that it is almost difficult to believe. I was told by a woman at a conference that in their agency a young woman with a disability was considered to have a problem precisely because she had a strong support network. She lived in an apartment having moved there from a group home where she knew a lot of people. After the agency made the decision to terminate all social activities for people with disabilities because segregated activities are wrong, immoral and sinful, her apartment became the social hub. She had friends over regularly and would host parties for her friends. Now all her friends had disabilities and this was a problem. The agency actually decided that she wasn't motivated to make, "real friends" (this is in quotes because it is actually what was said) and therefore she was ordered to stop all socialization with her "unreal friends." My opinion was sought. Should she be forced to stop socializing with other people with disabilities? When will people learn that when the question is force there is no dilemma. Force is wrong.

We need to celebrate the social networks that people have and then build on them. When we meet a person with a disability who has any social contacts at all, we need to ensure that we don't get in the way of their friendships. We also need to learn that people without disabilities are no more desirable as friends than people with disabilities. Those who are good friends are those who listen, support, laugh, cry, celebrate, understand and care. The ability level of that person is irrelevant for it is the strength of the heart that makes a friend, not the strength of the intellect.

✔Respect Support Networks. Sometimes I think that we have become so locked in to programming and teaching people with disabilities rudimentary skills that we forget both the artistic and spiritual side of the individuals that we serve. I have on my wall several pieces of art that were created by artists with disabilities. One piece of art I own was painted by a man with quite a severe disabililty. I was told that he becomes lost in his art. One of the few completely independent acts he performs is getting out his art supplies to draw or paint. He often did this when he was upset or depressed. For him his artistic muse was part of his support network. I've heard many staff mock art and its role in a person's ability to cope, I've even heard a staff refer to art therapy as "basket weaving 101."

We need to develop a respect for anything that provides support for a person with a disability, or any one of us. The following story I wrote and published in a couple of magazines, one for parents and one for Christian services. I wrote it because I believe that people need a full range of support. I print it here, aware that some reviewer will say that there are too many references to religion in this book, because I believe that if faith and family are part of the support network for people without disabilities, shouldn't they also be an option for people with disabilities? I know of both Christian and Jewish support services wherein people with disabilities develop a spiritual sense of self and a depth of faith in God that I envy. To me this is an option that should never be overlooked.

Of Community, Of Prayer, Of Welcome

Sadness. When I looked into her eyes I could only see sadness. We spoke after I had done training regarding self esteem and people with disabilities. She told me that she was both a professional and a parent and as such, had lost perspective. Someone who didn't know the situation would be a good sounding board. I was chosen. Telling me of her daughter her eyes changed as the slow flicker of pride lit up eyes that had cried to often. "My daughter," she said with a mother's warmth, "has done so well."

I was told a bit of the journey her daughter had

made. It began with an announcement by the doctor who first held her and who first rejected her. Mother was told that the child would "be" no one and would "become" nothing. The child who had no future was now a young teenager and was of age to join her faith community. She had studied hard and was ready to go through the Bat Mitzvah. The pride that first lit her eyes now filled her voice. Then she said that she had a question she wanted to ask me. Her mother had told her that she, as the child's grandmother, disapproved of the child going through a religious ceremony and being put on display for all the world to see. She turned away from me, crying, and asked if that's what I thought she was doing.

I told her that I did think that she was putting her child on display. She looked back at me in surprise, "I didn't think that you would see it that way." I told her that I did and more than that I thought that all parents who love their children want to put them on display for the world to see. The Bat Mitzvah, as I understood it, was an initiation and entry into the community as such it was a ceremony of welcome. Her daughter had a right to the welcome and the community had the right to receive the child as a woman. We also spoke of the fact that the spirituality of people with disabilities had been ignored. She told me that without her faith she would never have made it. She said that at times the only way she could turn was up. To her a support network went beyond family and friends and included faith. I asked her what the rabbi had said.

For the first time, she smiled. She said that the rabbi was wonderful and had told her of his first synagogue. When he came to worship he saw a man with a developmental disability deep in prayer. The man came regularly and prayed fervently. The rabbi had seldom seen such depth in faith. One day he kneeled beside the man to hear his prayer. He was surprised to hear the man repeating the alphabet over and over again. When the prayer was finished, the rabbi asked why he said the alphabet. The man with the disability said that he had worked hard to learn the letters of the alphabet but he couldn't learn the words of prayers. He then decided that he would just say the letters and let God make up the words. The rabbi told her that he would, without hesitation, perform the Bat Mitzvah.

She shook my hand and said, "You and he are both right. I am proud enough of my child to stand and say that she is mine. And my rabbi knows that God is proud of all that is made. We have made our journey, my mother must make her own." She left the hall. A mother who loved her child. A rabbi who wanted to welcome. A child with a God, a family and a community. I stood in the quiet and I tried to think of words to say in prayer of thanks for women like this one who love their children through all times and every adversity. What words can convey thanks to God for all the parents who love their children not only as they are but for who they are? How do you thank a community for wanting to welcome a child that a grandmother has yet to accept? Then the prayer came...

ABCDEFGHIJKLMNOPQRSTUVWXYZ

3

THE A.B.C.'S OF BEHAVIOUR

Quentin Crisp is an amazing storyteller and when he was in Toronto doing a show just down the street from me, I went. He was hysterical as he talked about style and developing a sense of personal uniqueness. One of the examples he gave was of a woman that he had read about in the London newspapers. She was a woman who was arrested for public nudity. Now in reading this, I ask you, is an arrest the appropriate consequence for public nudity? Some of you would probably immediately say, "Yep, you bet, swing your privates in public and jail is the best place for you." Others may hesitate. Well, when in court the judge didn't care about the *behaviour* what he cared about was the *context* and as such she was asked to explain herself.

She was a bag woman who picked through the trash in downtown London and the day of her arrest she found that there wasn't much in the way of pickings in the trash so she sneaked onto the tube and rode to a suburban stop to finish her work day by browsing through higher class garbage. In one of the pails she found that a cocktail dress had been thrown out. She held it to herself and it looked like it just might fit. Stuffing it into her bag she was pleased that she had made the journey to the burbs. When she arrived downtown there was the rush and bustle that comes with the end of the work day. She was desperate to try on her new dress and headed for the graveyard behind one of the downtown churches for some privacy to change. When she arrived, she hid behind one of the larger monuments that indicated that even rich people die and if you can't take it with you, you can spend it to remind people, in a big way, that you were here. A roving police officer strolling through the graveyard saw someone behind the monument and when he investigated he found a woman engaging in public nudity. Without question and without hesitation she was arrested.

Having heard all this the judge asked her then to state what she was doing behind the monument and she replied, "Like all women, I was dressing for dinner." She was freed, without punishment, without admonishment and with an apology. While Quentin Crisp used this as an example of a woman with wit and style, I would rather look at the behaviour of the police officer and of the judge. The police officer saw a behaviour and gave that behaviour an immediate consequence. The judge, looking at the same behaviour, gave it an entirely different consequence. For the police officer there is a set of laws and a set of reactions to the breaking of those laws. To the judge there is a behaviour surrounded by events that may provoke a behaviour and without understanding those, there can be no decision as to the rightness or wrongness of behaviour.

Unfortunately, we who work in human services are more often like the police officer and less often like the judge. It is for this reason that I really like behavioural theory. Behaviourism asks that we pull ourselves back from focus solely on the behaviour and look at the behaviour in its context.

We have all, at one time or another, tried to alter or change our own behaviour. Perhaps even more often we have tried the same with others. These efforts often end in frustration and failure. I think this is because we don't do what the judge did, we prefer to fixate on the behaviour, our own or others. The fascination with the behaviour we wish to change is understandable, but leads ultimately to a narrow and truncated view of ourselves and others.

We begin to see ourselves as beings in relation to a behaviour, and at the most extreme we may see the behaviour as more important that we are! What we will do is move from trying to control a behaviour, to interpreting the behaviour as a fundamental character fault over which we have little power. This internalizing of the problem behaviour into a problem personality is the only way we can deal with the fact that it is so difficult to change. The difficulty is seen as evidence of permanence. "I'm just shy," becomes the way we explain the behaviour of stumbling over words when in a large group. "I'm just a tad paranoid," is the explanation for refusing to answer the phone without checking the phone number. "I have a bad temper," becomes the explanation (some would say excuse) for ripping off someone's head who looked at you a bit wrong.

The road to frustration is paved with many attempts to change behaviour. Anyone who has tried to diet, quit smoking, control temper or start exercising can tell you that even making a small behaviour change is very difficult. As adults, we have years and years of learning behind us that makes changing at best difficult, because we have the behavioural habit firmly entrenched in the patterns of daily living.

Human behaviour does not work with infallible

rules as does mathematics or physics. If only behaviour changed as a result of some preset formula! Imagine if just the realization that there was a problem and a desire to change it would work. It should logically. If I know that I smoke and that smoking is bad for me, shouldn't I just have to want to quit in order to quit? If I know that I eat too much and that none of my clothes fit any more, shouldn't the desire to lose weight be enough? It is obviously impossible to change behaviours with simplistic solutions.

It seems that it is easy to forget our own difficulty with changing behaviour when we apply ourselves to the dilemma of dealing with the behaviour of others. We revert quickly to "simplistic solutions." It is as if we think that a client with whom we work only needs to be told that there is a problem and that we want it to change and it will change. We spend a great deal of time counselling about the problem behaviour. We want them to understand the problem and to be able to verbalize reasons why they are in error and should desperately want to change. Finally, beleaguered, the client accepts responsibility for their behaviour and promises never ever to do it again. Victory! We have done our jobs well. But then we find that the behaviour does not change. Now instead of having a happy but overweight client, we have a guilt ridden overweight client. This is progress!

Two things really attracted me to behaviourism, the first was a respect for the behaviour being performed. I loved the idea that there was no such thing as a bizarre behaviour, there were just bizarre environments into which bizarre behaviours made a perfect fit. I loved the idea that maybe we as clinicians needed to respect the behaviour for the purpose it served and that figuring out that purpose was, "*Job One*." The second was how behavioural theory placed emphasis on understanding human beings in the context in which they lived. If we attempt to understand how people attempt to fit in and have some control over their environment, then we will have a clearer picture of what is going on. In fact, behaviourists spend little time talking about the behaviour they are, like the judge, much more interested in talking about context. For a behaviourist there are three component parts to a behaviour. In effect the behaviour is seen as the action that follows an antecedent and precedes a consequence. Each of these needs to be understood.

ANTECEDENTS *(the PFFT)*

Have you ever noticed a dog, lying asleep, suddenly leap six feet in the air, feet running when it hits the ground? If you have you would know that the important thing is not the dog leaping, but the "pfft" of air as it enters the hole the can opener makes as it enters into the vacuum sealed can. If the "pfft" did not occur, the dog would not leap from sleep to feet. Antecedents are exactly that "pfft" that brings about a certain reaction. Almost every behaviour, that has a behavioural solution, has a "pfft." There are two things to think about when thinking about the antecedents. The first is to discover a link between a set of events and a particular behaviour, the second is to discover how to establish an environment that is structured to be the "pfft" to all sorts of appropriate behaviour.

In fact, we naturally do this when we become ill or have some kind of physical symptom. If you woke up tomorrow morning and discovered that you felt kind of stiff, what would be the first thing to enter your mind, after "Ow! That hurts." I'll bet you would think, now what did I do yesterday that caused this? Your mind would run through a variety of activities until you found something that you think may have caused the sensation of pain. For me, once, I was embarrassed to realize that my morning stiffness resulted from several hours of exercising; I had to get up and change the channel on the television in a hotel that didn't have a remote. (This was a hotel in the centre of a city but the middle of the dark ages.)

Antecedents, then, are tremendously important in understanding behaviour. It is here that we begin to look carefully at the environment in order to discover what may prompt the behaviour, or what the behaviour might be a response to, or indeed what might cue the person to perform the behaviour. By scanning the environment, we often find than many changes can be made in the environment which will effect the behaviour itself.

At the beginning of the chapter, it was acknowledged that it is difficult to change behaviour. Let's start by taking a look at a common "problem" like obesity (I prefer terminal chubbiness -- or perhaps fatally full figured). Almost everyone has, at one time or another, tried to lose weight. Being problem oriented, the fixation was solely on the weight itself. Let's look at the antecedents to eating behaviour. If you walk around a tubby person's home you may find a number of cues to

eat. The pizza take out number tattooed to his forearm.
A listing of all late night food delivery places tacked up by
the telephone. Candy dishes set out throughout the house
like watering holes. Subscriptions to magazines entitled,
"Microwave Your Way to Chocolate Bliss" and "You and
Edible Oils". You may even find the bumper stickers,
"Nutrition is for Snobs" and "Fat is Where It's At" on the
back of the station wagon. It is obvious that this home is
set up to accommodate someone who eats a lot and has
come to identify himself as an over eater. By making
changes in the antecedents that promote a different style
of eating, one can actually make gradual changes (which is
quite patriotic as one wouldn't want to wreak havoc on the
farming economy by a crash diet).

The antecedent then is anything that happened
before the behaviour occurred. It includes cues in the
environment, the time the behaviour occurred, the place
where it happened, the people around at the time, the
event which may have sparked the behaviour, and the
actions of staff and other clients. Sometimes, not often,
behaviours seem to occur out of the blue. Here we may
have to dig a little deeper. Could there be a medical
problem? What medications are used? What is the
client's learning history?

Antecedents can be immediately obvious, like the
staff giving a demand, or require much more looking. The
look is worthwhile, however, because they can save a lot of
time. One situation which was initially puzzling happened
when Giorgio moved from his parental home to a
community group home. Giorgio seemed happy and well
adjusted whenever he was visited at his parents' home. A

behaviour checklist was used to determine if there were any behaviours that the staff in his new home should be aware of before he moved. His parents stated that Giorgio was stubborn at times but was not a problem if someone took time with him. As English was his second language and he had difficulties with communication, staff who visited him and were preparing him for the move took a lot of time with him. He made several visits to the group home before moving. His visits would begin on a Saturday morning so that he could join in on week end activities and thereby meet the other residents. When he went home, usually in the early afternoon, he seemed to have had a good day. Everyone was hopeful that the move would go smoothly.

When the move happened, everyone was quite happy about it. His parents had the normal separation anxieties that all parents have when children leave home, but other than that, things went smoothly. But not a full day passed before there was a major problem. It happened at dinner time. He yelled, in Italian, at the staff and banged his plate on the table. The staff removed him from the table, sending him to his room without dinner. They wanted to let him know that this behaviour was simply unacceptable. Giorgio's parents were mortified. They had him come home right away. A meeting was held and it was decided to continue the move but to be more sensitive to Giorgio, as pretty much everyone agreed that the temper tantrum must have been a result of the move.

The next dinner at the group home resulted in the same tantrum. One of the staff noticed that this was the only time there was a difficulty. He seemed to like his new room, his new housemates, the new and increased activity level. It just seemed to be dinner. It was decided to invite Giorgio's parents, along with Giorgio, for dinner to help smooth out that last bit of difficulty. Upon arrival, they noticed immediately that the table was fully set and the salad bowls were placed, full on the table. They asked the supervisor if they had misunderstood dinner time and had missed the meal. Confused, the supervisor stated that the meal had yet to begin. It became clear, because of parental assumption that the meal was over, that Giorgio may be making the same assumption. The parents explained that in their home, in their culture, they ate salad at the end of the meal. The salad signified that the main course was finished.

Here, the culture of the individual had not been taken into consideration. There was agreement reached by the residents at the group home to hold "Italian Month" wherein traditional Italian foods would be eaten and served in the traditional Italian manner. It was seen as an opportunity to teach the others in the group home that there are other cultures with other ways of doing things, and as an opportunity to provide a meaningful welcome to Giorgio. A simple change of antecedent, the bowl of salad on the table, made further programming unnecessary.

This simple example illustrates an important point about antecedents. Taking the time to sort out what may be cueing a behaviour saves a lot of collective pain along the way. This has been seen over and over again. From finding that otitis media (a painful ear infection) was the antecedent to acts of destruction (turning work tables over) to finding that a client's medication was having a paradoxical effect (provoking the behaviour it is supposed to suppress) antecedent checks have been very important to understanding the nature of a behaviour.

Antecedents are more than observable events. They can also be internal or emotive events. These antecedents are much more difficult to pinpoint as often clients don't have the language with which to discuss feelings. When you think about your own behaviour, you will probably recognize that when you try to explain to someone why you did something mean, hurtful, spiteful, or nasty (yes, you -- go ahead and admit to the occasional lapse of control) how did you explain it? Perhaps you say things like, "I was just so tired," or "I had had a really bad day," or even "I don't know why I hurt you, I'm feeling just so confused.'" Now you know that none of these can take away the hurt from the other person but you want them to understand what was going on inside of you. These, oddly, make more sense and are more likely to gain sympathy and forgiveness from the "hurtee" than if you explain it by saying, "Gee, I'm sorry I called you the Warthog from Hell, but, listen a car cut me off in traffic." Even though an observer can see that such an event causes all sorts of language, it is less likely to be accepted by the "hurtee" (wart hogs being notorious for thin skins under all that hair) than an explanation of an emotional nature.

We need then to recognize that antecedents are both external (the car cutting me off) and internal (a feeling of being overwhelmed) and that both cause certain behaviours to occur. It can become such that when you see a particular behaviour in a particular person one can predict that a particular event has happened. I know that when I get home the adoring eyes of family, the solicitous requests for me to discuss what happened while I was away, the gentle prodding of me into my favourite chair while a cup of tea is being proffered, all this will disappear when the suitcase is opened and the presents distributed. All of a sudden it will be back to the "get your own tea fat boy," attitude I cope with on a day to day basis.

Years ago, I read a study which showed that children in North America were more likely to temper tantrum on the quarter hour rather than half hour or hour. Well you know that whenever there is a pattern there is an antecedent. Now why do you think that kids would be temper tantrumming on the quarter hour? Think about it for a second. Now, what could it be? Does the word television come to mind? Yep, it had something to do with how television has come to schedule a typical home. During commercial times it was discovered that family members actually spoke to one another. Now, do you think they are discussing world affairs (What has Princess Di been up to lately?) local affairs (What has the neighbour's wife been up to lately?), personal affairs (What have *you* been up to lately?)? Nope. What they found is that parents were shoving all the demands into commercial time. During that couple of minutes kids were expected to brush teeth, change into pj's, do last minute homework, make parents a snack -- how about a little crème caramel? Kids, surprise, surprise, acted out when this happened. Now we have a sense as to what is going on here.

Let's take it a step further. Instead of just imagining what it must be like *for them*, let's imagine what this would be like *for us.* I know in my own home, where we have an equal opportunity policy, when it is my night to do the dishes, if I am watching my favourite television programme and I get the little prompt, "Dear, don't forget it's your night to do dishes," it annoys me right proper. In fact, I usually have a two word response to the request. (I can't tell you what it is but I can tell you that one of the words is a verb!) I don't like it when that kind of thing happens to me. Let's put this in clear terms, the parents are inserting a non preferred task into a preferred task. Let's now empathize with the child, "I don't like it when someone inserts a non preferred task into a preferred task so the kid probably won't like it either." Now give suggestions.

When I do this in workshops for parents or professionals, not one in over six or seven thousand (I am not exaggerating) people have ever suggested punishment. Let's look at some of the suggestions that people make:

▸ Use natural breaks in the programming to actually talk. (Radical and unrealistic but a nice thought.)

▸ Restructure the evening to have the preferred task follow the non preferred task. "First you wash your hands then you can watch television."

▸ Establish a routine so the kids know what tasks come when so parents don't need to be constantly prompting.

▸ Have the non preferred task follow the preferred task. "After the programme is over, you need to wash your hands."

▸ Change the routine at the end of the evening by shutting off the television and doing some other family oriented "slow down" activity. (What kind of communist would suggest such a radically unAmerican approach?)

▸ Change the bedtime! It doesn't have to be on the hour or half hour. (This is more radical than you think, it's incredible how we will come up with a changeable structure or routine and then adamantly refuse to change it.)

▸ Don't allow the television to artificially rule the scheduling. One parent at a workshop said that in her home the last programme that they watch is something that she tapes during the day. The kids are allowed to watch the first half, then she pauses the programme and says that she will turn it back on when all the kids are washed and ready for bed. She says that she learned that her children can move really, really fast.

You will see by looking at the list above that an understanding of antecedents leads automatically to a restructuring of the environment into one that solicits appropriate behaviours rather than one that punishes and programmes. This is probably the best part of behaviour therapy because it asks us to be gentle and understand that all behaviour serves a purpose. In fact, people who understand always choose to prevent rather than punish.

Try a little exercise
(No, not the sweat kind - Who do you think I am Richard Simmons?)

I am going to list some behaviours and then I want you to try to think of the times that you perform these behaviours. I want you to think about both external and internal antecedents for when you do these things.

Behaviour	Internal Antecedents	External Antecedents
Swearing at a total stranger		
Refusing to do the dishes		
Kissing someone you don't know		
Banging your fist on a table		

Go ahead, make a list. I'm waiting. OK, now take a look at the process you followed. Ask yourself which was the most difficult to do. Most people find coming up with the internals much easier than the externals. Now take a look at what you did in your antecedental search. First, you scanned what would be happening around you and then what was happening inside of you and came up with a list. This is *exactly* the process that you need to follow in determining which antecedents may be in play for a person with a disability.

Caution

Please do not confuse the word "antecedent" for "excuse." An antecedent can explain the circumstances that prompt a behaviour but they *do not make violent or hurtful behaviour acceptable.* There is simply *no occasion* under which hurtful behaviour becomes acceptable. Once when reading about the atrocities committed by Jeffery Dalhmer gruesome detail after gruesome detail was presented regarding the murders and the victims. At the end the writer stated that given that Dalhmer was probably abused as a child it was *understandable* that he committed these crimes. PARDON ME? Am I alone here or is it possible to understand an antecedent without giving licence for people to become outrageously nasty? Oops, I ended up on that damn ol' high horse again.

BEHAVIOUR (the jump)

It is hard to grasp the idea that the actual behaviour that someone performs is of little use to an understanding of what is going on. Many people mistake "behaviour" for "meaning" and assume that a certain behaviour is clearly indicative of a particular meaning. But if that were true then humans would have never needed develop speech. Let's take a behaviour...

JOHN HIT

now what do you know about John? Is John Aggressive? Is John angry when he performs this behaviour? Is John frustrated? You realize of course that you don't know the answers to any of these questions. In fact, you don't know who John hit, why he hit them and whether or not the hitting was an appropriate response. So for understanding behaviours, the behaviour is of little use.

As you know the important thing is not that...

JOHN HIT

but the context in which the hitting occurred. Let's take a look at two very different scenes that allow us to know about how the antecedents have a play in determining our understanding of the behaviour.

Antecedent   Behaviour

Staff asked John to do a chore   **JOHN HIT**

Compared to:

Staff held up palm for a high five   **JOHN HIT**

I think you would interpret the hitting very differently from just understanding the antecedent (and think we haven't even gotten to the consequences yet!!)

The more interesting question in understanding behaviour is not "What did the person do?" but "Why is it inappropriate?" When we look at behaviours we have to understand that a behaviour is never inappropriate in and of itself. It becomes appropriate because of the context or because of the performance. Confused? Well, we have already covered context and how it makes a behaviour appropriate or inappropriate, let's look at performance.

To do this let's take "handshaking" as a behaviour. We can all agree that handshaking is a perfectly normal socio-sexual behaviour, can't we? OK, now let's take a look at when handshaking becomes inappropriate. There are four boundaries across which a behaviour becomes inappropriate:

Frequency

When someone shakes your hand every couple of minutes. This is annoying, tedious and will eventually drive you to distraction.

Alternately, when someone refuses to ever shake your hand, this is a social problem.

Intensity

When some bone crusher out there grabs your hand so hard you are almost taken to your knees. (This person is usually male and usually making up for a deficit elsewhere on his body.)

Alternately, when someone shakes

your hand in a very weak grasp. My father taught me that you had to shake hands firmly but without hurting the other person. (Hey Dad, bet you thought I wasn't paying attention!)

Duration | When someone holds on to your hand too long it becomes very uncomfortable. At one point you will stop listening to them and just start thinking, "Let go of me, let go of me, let go of me..."

Alternately, when someone drops your hand a second after touching it, you can feel as if you are dirty to the touch.

Discrimination | Ah, we are back to context. When, where, with whom and under what conditions the handshake occurs. One fellow we worked with had learned one greeting skill, hand-shaking, and ended up getting arrested attempting to forcibly shake the hand of the man next to him at the urinal. He had to learn that there is only one thing you shake at the urinal and it is not the hand of the man next to you.

So in considering a behaviour one needs to look first at

context and then at performance. But there is more to it than this. First, let's clarify something. Ask yourself this question, "What is a behaviour?" This is more difficult than it may first seem. In fact, when people think they are talking about someone's behaviour they usually aren't.

Take a look at the following conversation between two staff at shift change:

"Hey, Dru, what kind of shift did you have?"

"Don't ask, Neil. I'll tell you Lily was completely out of control."

"Not again!? Did she throw a tantrum?"

"A tantrum, the paint peeled!! In fact it so upset the other clients that Nathan freaked out and Olivia just got emotional. I thought that Malcolm was gonna act out."

"Wow, Dru, are you alright?"

"Thanks for caring Neil. Yeah, I'm fine but we have to do something about those tantrums."

"No kidding, we sure do."

In looking at the conversation above, what do you know. Careful now. You realize that you know very little. You know some vague information, like Lily threw a tantrum (what's that?) Nathan freaked out (huh?) Olivia got emotional (pardon me?) and that Malcolm might act out (as opposed to "act in?") Other than that you don't have any idea what happened. Unfortunately, people tend to talk in "categories" rather than "behaviour." Listen again to the conversation of two people who are talking about behaviours.

"Hey, Dru, what kind of shift did you have?"

> "Don't ask, Neil. I'll tell you Lily broke two windows."

"Not again!? What happened?"

> "She began to scream at chore time, when we tried to calm her down she started throwing things at the window!! In fact, it so upset the other clients that Nathan ran to his room and hid. He was so upset that Keesha had to go in to calm him down. Olivia sat in the front room and cried. I thought that Malcolm was going to hit her because he started slamming his fist into his hands like he often does before striking out."

"Wow, Dru, are you alright?"

> "Thanks for caring Neil. Yeah, I'm fine but we have to do something about those tantrums."

"No kidding, we sure do."

Now you have some information. You now know exactly what happened and even can probably think of some ideas just from having some facts. The trouble with language is that just when we really need to be specific we become vague and a lot of meaning is lost. Learning to use language that "paints a picture" rather than language that"lets off steam" is difficult but necessary. No it isn't as satisfying saying, "Lily screamed at chore time," as saying, "she threw a paint peeler" but it's a lot more helpful.

The best way to know if you are using clear language is to apply the "can I draw" test. If you use words that you would be able to draw what happened then you are being clear. If you would have to ask even one question about the behaviour itself (rather than the context) then you haven't been clear.

Try to draw this ... Victoria lost control at her job placement. If you are like me you will draw something like this...

Now try to draw this ... Victoria ripped up an entire sheaf of paper at the office. (Lucky for her she was wearing tasteful earrings....)

Humm, that should be a little easier, it would look something like this...

Now you have to admit that this picture looks a lot like the sentence, "Victoria ripped up an entire sheaf of paper at the office." So if you can't "see" it in your mind then you can't draw it, if you can't draw it then you are talking about a behavioural category rather than an actual behaviour.

So why is this important? Well, let's take a look at a young woman who was referred for being aggressive (can you draw this?) now when we checked it out we found out that she would, you guessed it ...

Hit

... so we put her on a program for hitting and then when we finished, closed the file, we felt satisfied. Then a few weeks later we got a referral because now she would ...

Spit

... so we put her on a program for spitting and then when we finished, closed the file, we felt satisfied. Then a few weeks later we got a referral because now she would ...

Bite

... so we put her on a program for biting and then when we finished, closed the file, we felt satisfied. Then a few weeks later we got a referral because now she would ...

Kick

... so we put her on a program for kicking and then when we finished, closed the file, we felt satisfied. Then a few weeks later we got a referral because now she would ...

You can see this could go on forever. Now what was the mistake? Well, I thought that the problem was the "behaviour," the problem is not the behaviour but how it is performed. We have to understand first *WHY* a behaviour occurred and we get this from context and from category. For her, we learned that she would hit, spit, bite and kick as a form of aggression when she wanted to express her anger when at work and discontent. So the category is aggression and the behaviour is hitting. Why is this important to know? Well, I had seen the behaviour as the problem and was trying to reduce hitting and increase production. The program never worked because I was giving a skill from a *category* that is unrelated to the behaviour. I needed instead to say, "What *category* does the behaviour fall into?" Then, "What is wrong with how she is performing the behaviour?" For the answer to this I go back to, Frequency, Intensity, Duration and Discrimination and find that Hitting (like Spitting, Biting and Kicking) are too intense a display of aggression. Then, "What is an alternate form of the behaviour that can be performed within acceptable limits that is in the same category?" Now, I need to teach that.

This still isn't clear is it? Let's go to another example. A number of years ago I was asked to do a consultation at a segregated school for kids with developmental and physical disabilities. One little girl, Nina, had been causing her teacher both concern and damage. She was reported to be "a scratcher" and an initial enquiry told me that she had scratched the teacher, teacher's aide, bus driver, school secretary, school principal and the visiting nurse. The only people she had not scratched were the other pupils in her classroom. When meeting her teacher, I met a wonderful person who was concerned about Nina and wanted to help her learn to control her behaviour. This was wonderful, often behaviour consultants meet angry people who just want to get "rid" of the problem (person).

When asking why she thought that Nina scratched she said, "She's an attention seeker." Automatically, she put the behaviour (scratching) into a category (attention seeking) and by doing so saved an awful lot of work. Because behaviours communicate little, sometimes the most difficult thing to figure out is what category it belongs in, scratching could belong in the categories, aggression, frustration, even temper tantrumming. I would not have leapt to the conclusion that it was attention seeking. Now that we have a category, what's your next question. I really want you to work at this and therefore am going to put the answer in code. Using a reverse alphabet. That means that A = Z, B = Y, C = X and so on. This is to encourage you to think of all the questions that come to mind when trying to figure out what the next question is.....

XZM HSV HVVP ZGGVMGRLM RM ZMB LGSVI DZB ?

Now that isn't a question that leaps to mind is it? We tend to see whole categories of behaviour as being inappropriate -- but think about it really, what is wrong with attention seeking anyways? So the above question then makes sense. The teacher looked at me with surprise at the question and said, "No, I don't think so!" Ah, ha! So we have a young woman who has a "one word" vocabulary for seeking attention. What if we took that away from her? We would be doing something very very unethical. We need to honour the behaviour and then teach an alternate form of doing exactly the same thing.

What do we have here? We have a woman who seeks attention using a particular approach, now what is wrong with the approach? Wait, wait, don't think about the fact that it induces pain (although that is important), don't think about the fact that she is alienating everyone from her (although that too is important), go back to Frequency, Intensity, Duration and Discrimination. What's wrong with how she does it now? It's too intense a form of attention seeking.

Just by asking the right questions about the behaviour we are led to a solution. What is it? Well, clearly we need to teach attention seeking skills. We need to encourage her to use other methods *in place* of what she is doing right now. The question above is an important question because it told us that we have to do a lot of teaching. We tend to think that people with developmental disabilities have skills that they simply choose *not* to use. Well, we are now suggesting that maybe they don't have the skills in the first place.

A BREAK TO TRY THIS FOR SOMEONE YOU WORK WITH...

Let's just say that right now you are working with a guy that has difficulty with aggression (category) and they engage in face slapping (behaviour). The question is of course ...

XZM SV HSLD ZTTIVHHRLM RM ZMB LGSVI DZB?
(don't worry, I'm not doing this again, the proof reader threatened to quit and spell check blew up!)

If the answer is "No!" then you have teaching to do. If the answer is "Yes" and the other option is appropriate then you have to strengthen that behaviour.

BACK TO THE INCREDIBLY GOOD EXAMPLE THAT WILL MAKE EVERYTHING CLEAR....

So what are we to do? We decided to actively teach attention seeking. When talking with the teacher we decided to teach her tapping gently on the shoulder or upper arm as an appropriate form of attention seeking. We made a bunch of arm bands that were padded (cause we aren't stupid) that had a big black dot on them. Around the dot were the words "Attention Button." Then, after having had her nails clipped (cause we aren't stupid) we actually structured teaching sessions where the skill to be learned was appropriate attention seeking (yes, this is a social skill, and an important one). The teacher would take Nina's hand, gently guide it to the button and then turn and smile and chat with her.

At first Nina was very confused. Here she was, obviously getting a response she wanted but the behaviour was very new to her. The strength of her desire for attention led her to quickly try the touch with only minimal guidance. Success, now it was time to generalize the skill. We taught the teacher, the aide and all who had been scratched how to guide her hand to the appropriate spot and then how to reward the gesture. In days we found that she was using a new skill. And guess what!?! When the appropriate attention seeking went up, the inappropriate attention seeking went down, all on it's own!

We were all gratified to see that she was now able to choose a means of getting what she wanted without hurting anyone.

This is the best that behaviour therapy offers, it is a tool for teaching, and used correctly the issue of "control" or "forced change" becomes a moot point.

CONSEQUENCE *(the treat)*

OK, what do these three things have in common?

> *A peck on the cheek*
> *Forgiveness*
> *A romp in the hay*

All are possible outcomes of giving someone flowers at an unexpected time. Sometimes behaviours aren't performed because of a set of circumstances, they are performed towards a particular end. Anyone who decides to drive miles out of their way so they can go shopping at Zellers so that they can get Club Z points is performing a behaviour to get some hoped for reward. Typically we perform behaviours to either get something or get out of something. When I was growing up, one of my aunts used to come a visit once a year. Every night at dishes time Auntie Margaret would have to go to the bathroom. (She had the best trained bowels on the continent.) She would stay there until others had started dishes.

This became known in our family as "pulling an Aunt Margaret" and was referred to anytime that someone tried to get out of doing something they didn't want to do by performing some kind of "escape manoeuvre." This lovely phrase bit the dust the day, when Aunt Margaret was visiting, that I (cute little bugger that I was) used it to refer to one of Auntie Margaret's little trips to the white seat. I still remember the shock on my Mother's face, the mortification on Auntie's face and the creeping sick/silly feeling I had when I realized what had blurted out of my mouth. Anyways, this was my first exposure to "task avoidant" behaviour and I'm sure my career is directly attributed to Auntie's well greased bowels.

So when we look at the consequences we need to look at the two rules of consequences. They are of course:

Any behaviour followed by a pleasant consequence is more likely to occur again.

And

Any behaviour followed by an unpleasant consequence is less likely to occur again.

Wake Up! Wake Up!!

OK, OK, some of this is a trifle dull, but do you expect me to have a truckload of Aunties full of crap stories that I can pull out any old time? Give me a break. The trouble with these relatively simple rules is that they are very, very difficult to figure out when they are happening.

In Toronto, when I lived there, the traffic Gods came up with a brilliant idea. They put up these signs on the freeways. They worked in an odd way. If you were travelling over the speed limit when crossing some beam, the light would flash:

Too Fast!!!

Now the Government figured (if one can imagine the government actually thinking) that we drivers would go by the sign, set if off, and then immediately put on the brakes realizing we were doing something wrong. Well, whoever came up with this must have a huge dry cleaning bill. (I hear that stains caused from brain slowly dripping through earholes are costly to get out.) It didn't work in a spectacular kind of way. I tell you that corner became dangerous. Remember we live in a game show society; when the lights go off YOU WIN! We all whizzed around those corners like neurotics on uppers. They became dangerous.

The government is acting here like many parents act. They understand the rule but misuse it. I remember one mom of a little boy with a developmental disability. He was a pretty good kid but he loved to bug his mom. She could cope with most of his silly behaviour but she had a rule that was of utmost importance to her. "Don't touch the piano." This rule for her was very, very important. Well, when I would make a visit to the house when the kid was with the baby sitter, he did just fine. The babysitter who didn't care two whits about the piano also didn't have any problems about him touching it. But mom would arrive at the door to the house and Jack would rise from the floor. The key would go into the lock and a look of absolute evil would cross Jack's face. The lock would click back and Jack would toddle towards the piano. The door would open and Jack's finger would plunk down on a key. Mother would explode. (The reason they call it the *nuclear* family is painfully obvious.) Jack would grin gleefully.

Mom would talk about how she always showed him her disapproval and would sit him on her lap and tell him about how the piano was to be left alone. Jack would cry and then they would both go for some treat. Jack knew exactly what he was doing. He performed a particular behaviour knowing exactly what was coming next. He knew that this behaviour (piano touching) was so valued by mother that she would take time from her busy, busy day to deal with it. One can easily imagine mom arriving home and going directly from work stuff to home stuff without much time for Jack, unless he did something that would force her attention.

This, my friends, is positive reinforcement. When you use the word "reinforcement" please remember that it always means "to make stronger." In other words it increases the frequency or duration of a behaviour. The words "positive reinforcement" in conjunction with "behaviour" means "adding something in to increase a particular act." So in this case the behaviour (piano touching) is positively reinforced (getting mom's time and attention) and therefore we can predict that it is going to happen more often. Mom, like the government with the **TOO FAST** sign, was actually making the undesired behaviour stronger! The trouble with the two rules (that you yawned through) of consequences is that they work and not only do they work, we tend to use them wrongly.

It is important to understand "negative reinforcement" as well. Again the word reinforcement means "increasing a behaviour" but the word "negative" means "taking away or avoiding something aversive." Auntie's toilet trips were negatively reinforced because the behaviour (going to the toilet) avoided doing an unpleasant task (dishes). Often these things are difficult to separate out. Let's take an example from something I saw in the mall in Oshawa.

A father and son were walking through the mall and passing by a candy counter. (How I happened to be there is quite irrelevant. Well, you think I got this size by eating oat bran like my Aunt Margaret?) The son said to the father in a conversational tone, "Dad, can I have a chocolate bar?" Now to the untrained ear this is simply a question. To those who know children, this is not a question it is a predicament. The father, daring the fates, said, "No."

Now this kid was the best temper tantrummer I have ever seen in my whole entire life. He went from a standing position to a lying position without bending his knees. Whap! He was on the floor in a tantrum that makes one question why hunting season is limited to furry, quiet creatures who live in the woods. Father stood there and a little crowd gathered to watch. You could see their thoughts form in cartoon thought bubbles over their heads, "If mother was here he wouldn't get away with that." Father looked at the crowd, looked down at the fruit of his loins in a full temper tantrum and then grabbed a chocolate bar randomly from the rack and handed it to his kid. The kid then levitated back up to a standing position and it was over.

Let's look at this situation from the point of view of positive and negative reinforcement. Who was positively reinforced? Remember that means whose behaviour is going to increase because something was given to them? Well, if your answer is the kid ... you are right. What behaviour is going to increase? Temper tantrumming (to the quick reader -- temper tantrumming is of course a category, not a behaviour -- the behaviour in this situation was falling to the floor, screaming until even the mannequins covered their ears). And what was added in? The chocolate bar. Wonderful.

Now, who was negatively reinforced? I can practically hear you say "the father" with incredible confidence. Like I'm not going to notice that he is the only one who is left in the story. Yep, the father was negatively reinforced. Now what behaviour is going to increase? Chocolate bar buying. And what was taken away? Now before you answer, remember negative here means that something unpleasant or aversive was terminated or avoided. So what negative thing stopped? Yes, the temper tantrum stopped.

In this scene, both the father and the son got what they wanted. In other words their behaviour paid off. The son got the chocolate bar. The father got the tantrum to stop. Now you can tell already that this is not a healthy pattern and if it isn't changed then the child will probably grow up to be a politician.

Positive reinforcement is around us all the time. We see stores giving prizes, teachers giving awards, parents giving treats, governments giving... wait now, government giving, OK well let's stop there. There are reinforcers or motivators everywhere and pretty much everyone is familiar with them. Negative reinforcement is just as powerful and just as prevalent but a little more difficult to see.

Have you ever got into your car and immediately, before starting the car, put the seat belt on? You learned to do this through negative reinforcement. You perform a behaviour (seat belt putting on) to avoid an unpleasant or aversive reaction (the seat belt buzzer going off). Have you ever noticed a child whining until a parent gives in? Negative reinforcement. The child is setting up an aversive (whining) that s/he will terminate when given the desired object or outing. This is negative reinforcement and the child is using it effectively on the parent.

Look at the two following examples and see how the same behaviour can be used for two different reasons, you will note that this Antecedent, Behaviour and Consequence stuff is starting to come together....

IG EX 1:

Antecedent	Behaviour	Consequence
Staff is on the telephone	Paul hits Christine	Paul is talked to by staff

IG EX 2:

Antecedent	Behaviour	Consequence
It's choretime	Paul hits Chris	Paul sent to his room

Reading IG EX (Incredibly Good Example) 1: You will probably guess that the antecedent is that staff's attention was elsewhere and that Paul performed a behaviour that served to get him attention. Reading IG EX2: You will probably guess that the antecedent is that staff requested Paul to do a chore he didn't want to do and he performed a behaviour that would get him out of that task. Now the first is positive reinforcement (his hitting is probably going to increase because he got attention), the second is negative reinforcement (his hitting got him out of a task he didn't want to do and therefore he will probably hit at the next chore time. Too bad he didn't have an Auntie Margaret so he could have learned alternate ways to get out of chores!)

Once again we see that the behaviour is not all that important in determining what is going on. It is the context in which it occurs. But be careful, we can make a huge mistake by depending solely on *our view* of what is going on. All of what we have done thus far involves us trying to figure out what is going on and then make some changes in approach or programme that will help someone learn a new way of coping. All of this, then, has depended on *us* and *our analysis* of what is going on. Even with careful analysis we can get off on the wrong track and create greater problems than there were there in the first place. Again an example. Here is the ABC as done by a staff regarding Keemo's behaviour.

Antecedent	Behaviour	Consequence
Staff makes a demand	Keemo hits the staff	Staff removes the demand

Now in looking at this it is obvious, is it not, that Keemo is performing task avoidant behaviour, and more than that if the behaviour serves to get him out of the task he is being negatively reinforced. OK, that's clear. Now what would you do next? If you are thinking that maybe we have to work at a way of providing motivation (positive reinforcement) for him to do the task, we would have to say slow down, or as the government would have it....

Too Fast!!!

First we would have to figure out some other possible antecedents. Wouldn't you, for example, really like to know just how the staff made the demand? But even with a thorough check of antecedents we still would be missing something. What's that? The client's perspective! Take a look ...

Antecedent	Behaviour	Consequence
Keemo can't do the chore	Keemo hits	Inability hidden Shame avoided

You know, you could program Keemo until the cows came home and he still wouldn't do the chore, not because he doesn't want to but because he can't. No amount of reinforcers, no punishers, none of these will work. Many parents and teachers of kids with learning disabilities will tell you that many children *cope* with their difference through acting out, it is as if the person thinks, "I'd rather you think I was aggressive than know I am stupid." We need to at all times be aware of who is doing the analysis and remember that the fact that we are not the person we are analyzing, we are going to miss things. No theory about people in the abstract can adequately explain the behaviour of a person in the specific. Remember to ask!

4

REINFORCEMENT:
THE TEN COMMANDMENTS

The eyes go dim. The jaw slackens. Drool forms at the corners of the mouth. The pen loosens in its grip. What causes this? I call it the "praise glaze" and it usually happens when I start talking about positive approaches to behaviour change. People seem to think that the idea of reinforcement is something they have to endure from well meaning, warm and fuzzy, behaviour consultants before they can talk about what is really important. "How long can we lock him in his room for?" Oddly, people seem to think that praise and reinforcement is the weakest tool for changing behaviour and that punishment is the strongest. This is not true. Many of the people who "pshaw" praise and ridicule reinforcement are often the same people who buy seven cd's they don't want to get one they do.

I think a big part of our problem with praise is that we don't live in a society that is comfortable with praise. When was the last time you were pulled over by a police officer and congratulated for driving well? When was the last time someone turned to you in an elevator and said, "Good Hygiene!" When was the last time your agency told you that you were doing a good job? For most of us, life seems to pass by with little in the way of personal reinforcement. For even more of us the giving and getting of praise is difficult and embarrassing. When I was in university I had a professor who wanted us to experience learning. He issued us a challenge. We were to go an entire day being positive. Whenever something positive popped into our heads we were supposed to say it, following laws of decency knowing that announcing that a passerby has "bodacious ta ta's" is wildly inappropriate.

I didn't think much about this, after all I, like everyone else, see myself as positive. In the morning the experiment began. When I got to the university I was surrounded by people I knew, people I liked and some that I even admired. And you know? I couldn't say anything. It was uncomfortable and every time I started up to say something, social convention stopped me. Here I was with people I cared about and all I was allowed to do was joke and tease. I was leaving it up to chance that they knew how I felt about them. Frustrated, I went for lunch mulling over my difficulty. I then decided to *Just Do It!*

I discovered that one gets bizarre responses when praising an unsuspecting public. There are four responses. The first one everyone knows, *Denial.* I would compliment someone on their choice of shirt, sweater, blouse and I would get a reaction like I had hit them hard in the stomach. They would double over, grab their clothes and say, "This? THIS!! I HATE THIS." Or they would glance at whatever item I praised and say, "This, got it for two bucks at a garage sale." So in either event my taste was either bad or cheap. The second is, *Suspicion.* "What do you want from me?" It was like I was only praising them to manipulate them. The third? *Reactive Praise.* You know when you praise someone and they praise you right back? "Like your shirt." The response then is a quick body scan and they say right back to you, "Like your pants." The people who use reactive praise will go as many rounds as you will. The final, *Concern.* "Are you alright?" They will find a "positive you" odd and they may think you are headed towards some psychological abyss.

So, I learned from this. We have a great difficulty in both giving and getting praise. This has a result on our ability to praise people with disabilities whose behaviours (and sense of self) that we want to strengthen. I know when I talk about praise I can see the discomfort forming and in the back of people's eyes. I know they are thinking, "No one praises me for getting out of bed in the morning. No one praises me for getting dressed with my pants on frontwards. No one praises me for getting through the day without drawing blood." There is clearly the sense that "No one praises me so I praise no one." So it's back to, "How long can we deny her dessert when she acts up?"

Well, then, since people are so uncomfortable with praise, you can bet that those who use it have some trouble with it. Have you ever had someone praise you by saying, "That's great, you aren't late for a change!" Did you feel a warm fuzzy all over your body? No?! You mean you felt slighted and kind of made up your mind that the next time you wouldn't bother showing up at all! The tragedy here is that the person who praised you probably thought that they were doing the right thing. They probably read in a magazine somewhere that praise is powerful. And now you are "p.o'd" and they are thinking, "This praise stuff doesn't work." Well, it does work. But reinforcement and praise should come with a rule book! There are many rules about reinforcement that look at how you schedule it, how you pair it, and how you fade it. All these are important but the most important thing is to learn how to give it! There are ten basic rules for the use of praise and reinforcement.

Be Immediate

We all know how much we like to get immediate feedback. Anyone who has rushed to finish a report and then waited for two weeks for a supervisor to get around to reading it (and then another week to make a couple of really stupid suggestions so that they can take credit for your work. Like yeah, changing that comma to a period gave the report a whole new twist!) knows how annoying and counterproductive delayed reinforcement is. Look at why we would be using reinforcement. Remember, the idea is that we are use it to make a behaviour "stronger." Therefore we are doing a combination of teaching and motivating. In this case we have to remember that with a developmental delay, a person has difficulty in learning and making connections. So by making the reinforcement immediate you are ensuring that the person can easily make the connection.

Years ago I met a woman who worked at a group home. She became pregnant and went off to have the baby. When she returned to the workforce she looked tired and wan. I asked her how it was to be back at work. She flopped in a chair and said, "I have been looking forward to coming back to work for weeks. I can't believe how quiet it is here." The "here" she was describing was a home for several people with disabilities that, with radios, t.v.'s, fights, record players, was anything but quiet. She then asked if we could talk for a little bit. I said sure and then she got up and closed the door. She looked at me began to cry and said, "My baby cries all the time. I have had her to the doctor. I have had the nurse come by. I have talked to other parents. I am at the end of my rope." Her tears flowed freely, she looked away and then said, "For the first time in my life I can understand why some parents might hurt their babies."

STOP!!!

This woman is not an abuser. She is not a potential abuser. She is not a victim of past abuse. She is not a woman obsessed with power and control. She is not in need of therapy, she does not need to start climbing the requisite dozen steps. What she is, if she *is* anything, is honest. We have lied to parents. I get upset every time I see one of those ads on television that presents parenting as a walk through some blissful fog. Parenting is the most  emotional journey any person will ever take. Children, by their nature as untamed demons, push parents to the edge of sanity and then stand laughing as you teeter. I do not know a single parent anywhere of any child that has not considered tissue damage as a parenting option. We have made parents uncomfortable in talking about the stress of parenting because they may be labelled as abusers. This is a tragedy. When this woman is able to say, "I am teetering at the edge, help me." She is a good parent, not a potential abuser.

She asked me over to her place. We walked in, and until that moment I thought she had been exaggerating. I did not realize that babies could cry all the time. But know what? They can. They really can. I was in that house for only five or ten minutes before I wanted to do tissue damage to the baby. We went up to the bedroom and found the baby in the crib. Which was fine with me because it was behind bars where it belonged. The mom looked at me and said, "You always talk about 'positive reinforcement' (she said it in the same tone that people use when they say 'horse's patootie') so what would you suggest." We stood with screams echoing through the house. The kid just screamed and when she tired of screaming, she hollered, and when she tired of hollering, she howled, and when she tired of howling she shrieked. It was a bit like being at a grunge rock concert.

Remembering the concept of immediate reinforcement, we went over to the crib, placed a blanket on its side so that the baby could no longer see out. Then mom sat down beside the crib. We decided to reinforce the breath in. This baby, like most babies, hadn't learned to scream on the breath in. So when the screech died down and baby stopped for an instant to take in the quiet air, mom would look over the edge of the crib. As soon as the scream started the mom would disappear from baby's view. It took about five minutes before baby started to experiment with silence. In an hour we were up to five minutes of silence. The baby learned that the world was different under two conditions. Silence brought mommy, screams sent her away. This was a whole new scenario for baby, but it was learned very quickly.

Immediate reinforcement is a teaching tool. Remember the individual has to make a connection between their behaviour and something positive. If a little baby can learn because of a quick connection between quiet and attention, so can anyone with whom you work.

Be Consistent

I know, I know, you are sick to death of the word consistent. But I want to take a slightly different approach to consistency. I think that the most important aspect of consistency in the use of reinforcement is not consistency meaning after each and every time without fail, but consistency meaning across time and across person. Let's get just one think clear, consistency after each performance of a behaviour is impossible. Consistency across time and person is quite possible. It is vitally important that people with a disability get the same message from people in all environments.

So then, of the two types of consistency, one is impossible and one possible. Let's look at both. For consistency after each performance of a new behaviour that you want to strengthen, it helps to realize that there are going to be occasions where you miss. We need to aim at getting 100% of the occurrences at first, knowing that we will fail. What this means is that we have to maximize the time that staff have to notice and reinforce the behaviour.

If you are, for example, trying to teach Rick a new way of expressing his anger and want to be able to provide consistent reinforcement for him when he gets it right, then you are going to have to make time for staff to do this. One of the things I realized early on is that "staff aren't bad people staff are busy people" now this may not be much of a surprise but some agencies explain their client behaviour by staff and staff attitude. I have found that staff only have poor attitudes if agencies don't provide them with the support they need. Usually when working with someone who is aggressive staff have been hit, smacked, spit on, knocked about, sworn at and even bitten, and then we come in an tell them that they need to increase the amount of time they spend with the person when that person (their victimizer) is "being appropriate." Well, hold on here. We need to acknowledge that this is going to be difficult.

We begin by looking at some time management. If Rick needs to learn a new way of dealing with anger then we want to ensure that staff have the time to teach and reinforce. This means that you are going to have to look at all the responsibilities that staff have and get rid of some of them. Maybe some of that paperwork isn't so important, maybe Blade's hand washing programme can go on hold, maybe Ashley's shoe tying programme can be shelved for a little bit, so that staff have the time to do what needs to be done. WOAH!! Boy do I hear a reaction. Millions of readers, OK, hundreds of readers, OK, you, just thought, "Hey, why should Blade and Ashley have to give up some of thier time? Just so that jerk Rick can 'learn more appropriate ways of expressing his temper.'" Well, let's just look at this situation from the point of view of Blade and Ashley. If I were one of them living in a house with someone like Rick who hits people, throws furniture and generally causes mayhem, I would probably be stressed out constantly. If you asked me I would say, "Sure take my hand washing programme and use that time to work towards an environment wherein I feel safe." Remember if you have someone who is acting out in a group living environment, the staff get to leave after a rough shift but the other people with disabilities can't look at their watch and say, "OK, I've been around an out-of-control violent man for 8 hours, think I'm going to go for a beer." Nope, while you are slugging back a frosty one, their stomachs are still tight and they need sleeping medications just to get through another day of tension. So no, I don't think it is unfair to take the time needed to work with someone who is causing a lot of problems. And neither do Blade nor Ashley.

The other kind of consistency, across person, is achievable but boy can it be difficult to do. The interesting thing about us in human services is that we all hate each other. You should hear the residential people talk about the vocational people (they don't care about the people they just care about production). You should hear vocational people talk about residential people (What are they thinking sending a person in to work looking like this!). This schism causes problems because we just don't talk to each other. In order to be consistent across place we actually have to meet and talk about the behaviours and skills we want to make stronger in someone that we are working with. Ooooh, there's a scary concept, talking with one another when there isn't a crisis.

Be Specific

Remember, praising is teaching, praising is teaching. If I came up to you and said, "Wow, you sure are doing well." What am I praising you for? Reading this book (very good), sitting quietly (nice sitting), doing your hygiene (you did didn't you?), wearing clothing

appropriate to the circumstances (you are aren't you?).
Well, in fact you don't know and neither does anyone else.
As a motivator I would be failing you, as a teacher I
would be failing myself. It is my job to provide encouragement, motivation and information all in a couple of
seconds. Even though praise should be used consistently
through someone's life, we use it as a *tool* when we are
attempting to build someone's skill base. As such we then
have to realize that the only reason we are doing this in
such a concerted way is to ensure that someone is learning
something new. So it only stands to reason that we
become very particular in what we say, so let's take a look
at the three component parts of a praise statement.

First, we have to tell them *what* they did. Remember you are teaching someone, you don't want them
to have to guess at what you mean. Second, you have to
tell them *why* what they did was important. Third, you
have to tell them how you *feel* about what they did.
Sound complex, well, it really isn't. Take a look at the
following praise statement...

"That's great you hung your coat up on the hook, the
hallway is neat and clean and I feel proud of the house
when people come in."

That only takes 4 seconds (approx) to say. I know
this because I timed myself saying it on my Timex Indiglo
watch. (Hey, how about an endorsement deal? Timex?
I'm waiting.) But look at the information that is included
in one 4 second (approx) statement. First, you know what
was done. The slobby little bugger actually managed to
hang up his coat.

Second, you know why "coat hanging behaviour" is important. This may seem obvious to you but let me tell you there is nothing inherent in coat hanging behaviour that communicates a sense of "why-ness." I come from a background wherein where (my mother hates me writing about this stuff) we never hung coats up in the hallway. Are you kidding? We would strip off our coats, pitch them on the dining room table, and head on into the house. For us, dinner was served on TV trays while watching the exploits of a nun that could fly, a witch that flicked her nose and *cousins, identical cousins,* on the television.

If I moved into a group home as a child and you were making me actually hang my coat up, I would feel resentful, bitter and would fight you over the issue. A real surprise hit me when I started doing more counselling of people with disabilities. I discovered that they thought we were just mean. Plain old, flat out, mean. They didn't understand the "reason" behind so many of our *orders, demands and requests.* I think that you and I have learned the "why" and kind of figure that it is self evident and therefore don't feel a need to explain ourselves.

Think of an absurd, meaningless, obsessive compulsive behaviour that people perform without much thinking about it, like, say, making a bed. Now I believe that the world is broken into two groups of people, those who perform this slightly odd behaviour and those of us are free of such demands. I am willing to bet that those who fall into my category, were brought up by people who had the "because I said so" approach to parenting. To me, "because I said so" is a reason to rebel not a reason to comply. In fact it isn't a reason at all it is a statement of parental authority and power. The others, the "bed-makers" of the world, I am willing to bet were brought up by people who explained and requested rather than demanded and set up opportunities for power struggles at every turn. So, please admit that most tasks don't communicate somehow through performance their rationale. That's your job. The praise statement makes it clear that the behaviour has a purpose and effects the world in some way. More than that it leads directly to the third part of the praise statement...

How you feel about it. Stating that you have an internal feeling response to a behaviour is probably the most powerful part of the praise statement. An individual working to learn a new behaviour, a new way of controlling temper, a new way of handling disappointment, a new way of putting a shirt on, needs to know that their effort, their success and their willingness to try has a positive effect on you. Stating that you feel pride, you feel happy, you feel excited, you feel warm and gushy inside, when someone experiences success is important.

It interests me that I have such opposition to this part of the praise statement. People actually come up to me after a presentation and say that they took a course on being positive and learned that it was inappropriate for professionals to tell someone with a disability that they feel proud of them. Apparently, I am told, statements of pride are inappropriate because it denotes ownership (it does?), it demeans the "other" (really?) and that it takes away from their own sense of accomplishment (huh?).

I totally disagree with these sentiments. I find the idea that we should not express positive feelings repugnant. One of the most emotional things I have done in workshops is ask members of an audience to put their hands up if they would remember their childhood better if they heard their parents say just five more times, "I'm proud of you." The response is extraordinary. Almost everyone does. Apparently all these people in the audience had parents who had been warned of the danger of saying "I'm proud of you." And there they sit still desperate to hear that they had occasioned the sense of pride in their parents.

I admit that to this day I have never heard the words, "I'm proud of you" from either of my parents. I have heard it from aunts, uncles, friends, strangers, but never my parents. And anyone who says that the word 'proud' is dangerous is right, but only when it is *not* used. So, feel free to let people know that they can make you feel proud. Remember, if you needed it more and you are a respected professional, then imagine that a thirty-some year old person with a developmental disability may never have heard it at all. I can attest to how that feels. And given the discussion I have had after many workshops, maybe you can too.

Give Praising Praise

We hate praise in this society. I really think we do. In fact, I find that often instead of praising people we package criticism into a nice box. Have you ever arrived at a meeting and had your boss say, "Well, wonderful, you aren't late for a change." Do you feel a warm fuzzy all over your body? Do you drop your eyes and demurely say, "Why thanks, what a good and wonderful boss I have to notice little ol' me." Or do you feel like punching the @#$%^*?

Well, I think we do this a whole lot. We need to give people real praise, praise that is actually positive. While this may seem simple, it often is very difficult. Many people like to praise people for what they *didn't* do. For example, have you ever praised someone by saying "That was good you went to the mall without causing a couple thousand dollars damage." Or, "You didn't hit Lynne at dinner, good for you." In both these cases you are commenting on what the person *didn't* do. Think about what is going on, first, just like you being reinforced for not being late, it just doesn't feel particularily reinforcing. And second, it just may prompt the problem behaviour.

Often people have said to me that they have tried that "praise thing" and it didn't work, as proof they tell me that when they praise someone they immediately act out in "negative" ways. Well, I thought this odd, so I went to watch a young mom praise her child with a developmental disability for good manners. For this kid, good manners meant not using kitchen utensils as projectiles and actually swallowing the food rather than chewing, gooing and spewing. So there she was slowly coaxing and reinforcing her child for eating properly. After three spoonfuls of soup that were eaten with relative success, Mom said, "That's great, you didn't dump your soup." Immediately the soup was lifted and dumped. Mom glared at me through broth dripping down her forehead and said, "See, praise only set's him off!"

In looking at what happened, we see that Mom essentially said this to her child...

"Listen, you *SOUP DUMPER* you, I know that you didn't *DUMP* your *SOUP* today, but don't think I've forgotten that you are a *SOUP DUMPER* now and always will be a *SOUP DUMPER*, you *SOUP DUMPER* you."

...the child is learning that **SOUP DUMPING** is so important to Mom that she brings it up even when it doesn't happen. The child is learning to incorporate the label **SOUP DUMPER** into his basic self concept.

There can be a problem in figuring out what to praise someone for, because sometimes what they are doing is not particularly obvious. Someone asked me how to praise a person they were working with who had a particularly dangerous behaviour problem. This person loved to go for car rides but had very low frustration tolerance. When the car was moving she would sit quietly and watch the scenery go by, but when the car had to stop for a stop sign, a stop light, or for some traffic related issues, she would get upset. She would attempt to grab the steering wheel and would try to push at the accelerator. When they stopped and she sat for a couple of seconds quietly they would say, "Good sitting." Knowing that I was opposed to the "good sitting" style of reinforcement, I was asked how to praise her.

Well, first let's recognize that "sitting" is not the

issue. Why reinforce her for a behaviour that isn't really what you want? She probably sits many hours of the day and this sitting is quite unrelated to her not engaging in severe back seat driving. The issue here is "patience." If you can't come up with a "behaviour" that a person is performing, then praise the "skill" they are demonstrating. Turning to her in the car and say, "You are so patient. I like being in the car with you when you are so calm because it's safer and I enjoy it so much more." (Yep, the three component parts of a praise statement are there, and this one takes about 5 seconds. Timex, I'm waiting.)

Be Sincere

Have you ever tried to change your behaviour? It's tough isn't it? Well, then if we are going to try to teach someone a new skill or a new way of dealing with frustration, fear or anger, then we are going to have to pick something that we really care about. That caring will communicate in our praise. People need to know that we really do care and we really do appreciate the effort it takes to learn something new and to try to make a major shift in how they behave. One of the first things we need to learn is to reinforce effort over accomplishment. That is so important I'm going to set it out more clearly.

Reinforce Effort over Accomplishment

Remember that people with disabilities have failed a lot at learning. This means that when they attempt to learn some new way of doing something, they are probably predicting failure for themselves. You need to feel very honoured that they are attempting to learn again. This means that you have created a safe environment for them to even try to learn.

I remember seeing a sad situation in a group home. They were frustrated with Mamie. She had just given up. She was bored, listless and refused to try anything new. Motivation programs just didn't work and an anti-depressant just seemed to make her bear her boredom and inactivity better. The biggest problem they had was explaining in the annual meetings that Mamie just wasn't motivated. She wasn't meeting her potential, she wasn't learning skills in all of her domains. She was an embarrassment to the system. Well, one day when a new staff was hired, Mamie seemed to perk up. In fact John, the staff, seemed to really like Mamie and would spend time with her. She was more willing to participate in activities if John was going to be there helping out.

It was decided to use John's ability to provide motivation for Mamie and have him teach her the skills that she needed to learn in order to keep the government funding body quite happy. Vacuuming was the first thing they picked. I happened to be at a staff meeting when they were going to start so I watched John take her into the front room and get her to plug in the machine and then slowly with bits of encouragement finishing the job doing a reasonable job. When she finished she looked to him for approval and he looked over the carpets and said, "So you think you are finished, do you want me go get a flashlight so that you can see into the corners?" Her face fell, she dropped the vacuum hose and left the room crying. Last I heard she was still listless and unmotivated.

What he did was cruel. To be fair to him this is probably how he was parented, but to be fair to her, that doesn't matter. We all have to remember that when we are at work we are professionals who can short circuit our own programming and act in ways that actually build strength in someone's self concept. What he did was determine that praise would be given based on *performance* not based on *effort*. The fact that she made the *effort* was nearly miraculous, the fact that she failed in the *performance* was to be expected it was her first try. Our job is to get someone started, feeling secure, feeling like they want to try and then to increase their skill in performance.

Step One *Motivate* Step Two *Activate* Step Three *Educate*

These are three distinct steps. The problem is we usually attempt them the wrong way round. We usually attempt to educate, fail, then try to get them up, fail and then sit around in meetings trying to come up with this reinforcer, that token, this treat, that checkmark and wonder why the person doesn't leap to try again. It has always been my opinion that people with developmental disabilities have been told so often by schools, parents and systems that they are dumb and can't learn that they actually believe it. Our first step is to tackle that issue. When a person with a disability actually tries to learn something new there should be a brass band playing, a choir of angels chanting and a group of staff cheering.

Making sure that you are letting the person know that you really do care that they are trying, you really do notice their effort and that you really are honoured that they trust you enough to try this once more may be the most important part of your work with an individual.

𝕿𝖆𝖐𝖊 𝕿𝖔

What is reinforcement, really? Clearly it is more than just some words strung together stated after someone has performed a desired behaviour. Maybe it is even more than a grouping of positive words expressing pleasure that has its intent encouragement and the strengthening of a behaviour. Perhaps it's more than that. When you look at the dictionary, it says that reinforcement means, making stronger. That's nice, and I like it a whole lot more than how it is often referred to in human services. Well, I tend towards a poetic definition of reinforcement, what is it?? Prepare youself, how often do you get absolutely beautiful poetry in a book like this ... how good could it be?

Reinforcement is ....
taking success to where failure usually occurs

(Ok, I won't give up my day job)

Think about it, when you reinforce someone, the reason you are doing it is that they are demonstrating a new skill or a new way of coping and they are doing it in a place where they have failed in the past. By taking the reinforcement to the person you are giving them the opportunity to experience success right in the place where they had difficulty in the past.

When you were in school, did you ever have difficulty with a particular subject? One of those classes that when you began to walk towards the classroom a thin film of sweat formed on your back? Did you define a good school day as one where you didn't have to take that class? What if I could magically transport you back to that classroom? Do you think that just going into the room overwhelm you with feelings of failure? Would you be able to "hang memory pictures" on various walls of the room? Would you beg to get out of the room? Surprise, surprise, most of us have those memories (those that don't are now investment bankers living well off the backs of others) and most of us have places, spaces and faces that bring back unpleasant memories. For a person with a disability who has had difficulty either learning a new skill or a new way of coping you can bet they are surrounded by memories of past failure.

Years ago I got a referral for a young woman who needed to learn toiletting skills. I went for my first visit to the home and met with a wonderful woman who had been providing foster care to kids with disabilities for years. She was frustrated at her lack of success with teaching Leanna how to use the toilet. While we were chatting the door opened and Leanna came in from school. I noticed right away that she shied away from the bathroom door as she passed it in the long hallway. So much so that she pressed up against the opposite wall in order to get as far from the door as possible. This struck me as odd.

I went to her file and found that she had been in a small institution before making her way to foster care. They had attempted toiletting training, failing miserably.

At each failure they upped the punishment quotient and had ended by tying her on to the toilet for up to an hour at a time in punishment for toiletting accidents. This is not programming this is brutality. No wonder the poor kid was shying away from the bathroom, to her it was a place of failure, and beyond that it was a place of punishment and brutality. This was were we would start.

Clearly the goal is not toiletting, it is teaching her that she can be successful and that she can be successful in the bathroom. We began by talking about what Leanna liked. Her foster mom told me that she would often find Leanna hidden in the bedroom playing with a music box that she would "sneak" out of the front room. This was her favourite thing in the house. Mom offered, hesitantly but sincerely, to let us use the music box as a reward. I knew this to be a bad idea because if it were broken there would be hard feelings. But we thought about it and went shopping, and to our delight found that you could buy musical toilet seats!! I'm not kidding, we found one that played "Moon River" think about that little irony. We then let her play with it in other rooms in the house. She liked lifting the lid part and making the music play.

As this was going on we were still talking about the fact that she feared the room. Mom then went out and bought a burnt orange light bulb and placed it in the bathroom. Suddenly the room didn't look like a bathroom anymore. She changed the "sense" of the room in hopes that it wouldn't scare Leanna quite so much. A brilliant and caring idea, all our ideas should be this sensitive.

Finally we talked about getting success into the

room. Mom offered the idea that Leanna was very good at washing her hands and would do so before dinner at the kitchen table. Aha, now we can start. We put the toilet seat into the bathroom, be fore dinner (a natural reinforcer and motivator) Leanna would be asked to wash her hands in the bathroom. This wasn't a big struggle because of the new look of the room. She would go in, turn on the light bulb, lift the lid of the toilet seat, wash her hands, shut off the music, shut off the light and leave.

But. *BUT*. As soon as she finished with the hand washing she would get a mega dose of praise. She would be told that she was the best little hand washer in the entire world. Her hands would be rubbed and she would be congratulated for doing such a good job. Now, what are we doing? Clearly she already knows how to wash her hands. What we wanted to do was to use reinforcement as a means of teaching that *YOU CAN BE SUCCESSFUL IN THIS PLACE*. You *CAN DO IT*! We wanted her to see herself as someone who could learn in a bathroom and that bathrooms are places where learning can occur. Once we did that we then were ready to teach.

Take a look at some of the folks who are having difficulty learning something. Look at their faces, look at the faces of the staff doing the teaching. If you don't see there, in *both* faces an expectation that the person is going to succeed, then you are seeing an exercise in frustration not an exercise in education. We have to make sure that we have set the stage for learning to occur. This often requires that we step away from the immediate goal and create an environment in which the person feels that there is at least a slight chance that they can succeed. Without this, our education programmes are just another version of professional self stimulation.

Vary the Reinforcer

(For those, like me who have difficulty reading that typeface, it says, Vary the Reinforcer, not Bury the Reinforcer.) When I first became a behaviour consultant I was overcome with a sense of arrogance that was a tad overwhelming, to others, I barely noticed it. I was so sure that those damned front line staff would muck up all my fancy programming. I left nothing to chance. I would actually write down the praise statements that they were to use when an individual with a disability "earned a praise statement." Doing this I destroyed all natural inter-actions, I demeaned them as professionals, I demeaned people with disabilities by writing generic, one size fits all "reinforcers." When I went to watch my programs run, I couldn't quite figure out what was wrong. Then finally I had to admit that the question was not "what's wrong here," but "who's wrong here." The answer unfortunately was, "Me." I had taught people do to the three component parts of a praise statement. I even scripted their interactions, which sounded a lot different on paper than they did in the real world. It wasn't long before the staff, people with disabilities, and I was completely bored by the mechanistic manner that I had given them.

Look back at the component parts of a praise statement. Learn them well, they will serve you well. But please, please, (*PLEASE*) don't use them all the time. Use praise statements intermittently along with other positive interaction. Sometimes a well timed thumbs up, or a quick and spontaneous high five, or a smile is all it takes to get the message across. Routinized praise becomes real boring real fast. My mother taught me one social skill, the rest I learned on the streets, but the social skill she taught me is one of the most important and it is:

When you are bored you are boring!

There is so much truth in that. In fact, I think that the major problem that exists in the field of developmental disability is that everyone is completely bored. People with disabilities are bored by all the inane programmes they are forced to submit to. Staff are bored to death by all the inane programmes they are forced to run. But everyone goes through their paces. Well they say that variety is the spice of life, and you know it really is, really.

When I first moved to Toronto, I met a woman who was one of those people who constantly did the same thing over and over again. I told her once that I liked Turkish delight. Well, she would give me Turkish delight (I just realized that some of you may not know what Turkish delight is, you may be thinking that I am writing about some incredibly exciting sexual act. But sadly, no, Turkish delight is a kind of candy) just because I was special. Because it was Wednesday. Because in the winter the world tilts away from the sun. It got to be like finding little rabbit turds littered throughout my life. I grew to hate Turkish delight, the white paper and green ribbon she always wrapped it in and of course eventually, her.

We, none of us, like getting the same thing over and

over again. We like surprise. We like variety. We like the suspense of not quite knowing what comes next. The same should exist when you are providing a motivation programme for a person with a disability. Vary the reinforcer. Use words, signals, outing, special treats, and mix them all up. It will keep everyone interested.

Give it Time

One of the most amazing thing I have found in human services is the fact that we figure someone should change a behaviour just because we praised them a couple of times. We kind of figure that if we give a word or two of encouragement it should overcome years of negative messages. Yeah, right. We know that it takes time for us to make changes, but they should do it just because we want them to, we told them to, or we programmed them to. Well, it's not so easy.

I remember being at a meeting wherein we were discussing the FIRST WEEK of a positive program to increase someone's coping skills. One of the staff waited until I had taken a brief look at the data sheets and then said, "Well, we've done the positive stuff and it hasn't worked, I think it's time to consider something more effective." By "more effective" she meant of course something like time out or some other kind of punishment technique. It's interesting that the same people who don't want to get off their butts to give someone a bit of praise or encouragement are quite willing to leap into the air and pull a struggling and increasingly angry and upset person across a room and lock them into a little time out room.

This makes no sense to me, in fact, I attribute the fact that fat people are seen as jolly to the fact that we tubbo's figured out that nasty takes calories and happy intakes calories. Nasty means moving, happy means celebrating. Nasty means exertion. Happy means eating.

Suffice it to say that a person is going to have to learn the new approach, practice it a bit and then become comfortable with it. Just like you do. This takes time. One of the most damaging things you can to is run a positive program for too short a length of time. Every time you stop short of a goal you have to come up with a new approach and the person with a disability learns to distrust any programmatic attempt to help them. Why begin something if it's going to change in a week or two?

Be Fair

When using reinforcement with people with disabilities I often hear people say, "She just doesn't like anything? What can we use as a reinforcer when she doesn't like interaction, outings, treats?" This is a difficult question and usually it leads to a different kind of analysis, if someone has nothing they like in their life, they don't have a life. We maybe need to build some "pleasure skills" so that a person can get up in the morning expecting something more than drudgery and dreariness. We maybe need to recognize that some of these folks who "don't like anything" lived for years in institutions where they "didn't have anything." We maybe need to recognize that if we are programming someone using negative consequences because they don't have any positive likes, we are being a tad unethical and lacking a tad of compassion. When working with folks who have behaviour problems who staff describe as totally unmotivated, lacking any possible reinforcer in their lives, and constantly depressed and lethargic. Maybe we gotta think about that. Maybe we gotta take seriously all the earmarks of a significant depression. Maybe we gotta DO something about that first. Maybe.

One of the temptations that can befall us when working with someone who has few reinforcers is to use whatever presents itself to us. I actually ran a program years ago for a fellow who had a problem with anger, when he felt angry he hit whoever was near. In order to help him deal with his anger we wanted to teach him to talk about the anger rather than strike out. As part of what we were doing I actually decided to use his hat as a reinforcer. To say that he "liked" his hat is like to say I "like" breathing. He went no where without that hat. It was the last thing he took off when arriving at the workshop and the first thing he put on on his way out the door. He would make several trips to the cloak room to make sure it was still there.

So Dave, here, decides that this will motivate him. So, with his parents' permission (yeah like it was THEIR hat to give permission about) I took the hat from him and told him that he could earn it back after a day of showing control of his anger. The first few days were hell. He was angry all the time. The fact that he only hit a couple of times when dealing with moment by moment anger attests to him asserting control. He was miserable, he was angry, he was resentful, he was right. I had no right to take something from him and then allow him to earn it back. This is unfair and unethical. If we are going to do reinforcement properly we have to "give more". If I had decided that he could wear his hat at all breaks if he had showed control, I would have been doing reinforcement. What I was doing was depriving and then returning. This is control. This is power. This is wrong.

So when you are considering using someone's dessert as a reinforcer, stop and think about it. They already have dessert. You can't take it away and then give it back. An extra dessert now that's reinforcement. So be careful not to impoverish people for programmatic benefit. It may work, but it will never feel good.

Always respect

This is the last of the ten rules. I don't have the skill to describe, in words, respectful treatment. Looked up the word, "respect" in several dictionaries, here is some of what they said ....

Respect is ... show honour or courtesy to
Respect is ... courteous consideration
Respect is ... deference or dutiful regard
Respect is ... to hold in high regard or esteem

If this is lacking in your words, your attitudes, your actions, it will also be lacking in your programmes. Be careful.

WHAT KIND OF ZHHSLOV!?!

It was one of those kind of moments when you want to just shrivel up and die. I had been doing a consultation regarding a young man with a developmental disability. After meeting with him, observing him in his "natural environment" and discussing him at some length with the front line staff who support him, I was enraged.

The programme he was on was heartless and unfair. It was technically fine but showed no sensitivity to him, his living situation, the reality of staffing and funding dollars. It didn't seem to see him anything other than a being that could be controlled via a mechanistic arranging of reinforcement contingencies. More than that, it was just plain cold.

Listening to the staff describe their difficulty, ethically, in running this year old programme, my rage grew. Why hadn't these folks, who knew him best, been heard? Why had their obvious concern been shelved? My sense of outrage had to be vented. I used very impolite language and said, "What kind of insensitive, uncaring, *Zhhslov* could have written this programme?"

It was a moment that the front line staff rep had been waiting for and she capitalized on it. She looked at me levelly and said, "Why, it was you."

I was flabbergasted. Absolutely floored. Gasping for air like a blowfish out of water, I sputtered protest. But surely, no, I had never met him. I had never been to that agency. It couldn't be me!! I could not, would not, do that kind of programming.

It was revealed to me that I had met with their supervisor after a conference once and made a series of quick recommendations. This I barely remembered, but it must have happened, they showed me the meeting summary.

I had transgressed a fundamental rule. I had given advice for the treatment of someone I had never met. I had assumed that a brief discussion of data and data points, a quick glance at a graph, and a perusal of a one page report that begins, "Steve is a 23 year old man with a developmental disability," was all I needed to know.

Let me just remind you that the most important aspect of our work with people with disabilities is our relationship with them. Without a relationship filled with compassion, understanding, tolerance, acceptance and genuine caring, every professional who serves another is in danger of becoming unethical really quickly.

Funny thing is, once a relationship is developed, often the problem simply disappears. So before you do anything else, consider your relationship with the people you serve. Is it a healthy relationship wherein respect is felt and shown, wherein listening actually occurs, wherein time is spent just "being together," wherein control flows naturally back and forth between two equal parties, wherein power is something shared, wherein lives meet? If not, start there.

RESOURCES TO CHECK OUT

The Habilitative Mental Health Care Newsletter: A bimonthly Mental Health / Mental Retardation Publication. Subscription rates: US $49 personal, $63 institutional. Psych-media, Inc. PO Box 57, Bear Creek, NC 27207-0057

The National Association for the Dually Diagnosed. Memberships Ind $50. 110 Prince Street, Kingston, NY 12401 1-800-331-5362

Mouth: the voice of disability rights. Subscription rates: US $48 organization, $16 person with a disability. 61 Brighton Street, Rochester, NY 14607

People First International, Box 12642, Salem, Oregon 97309

TASH: The Association for Persons with Severe Handicaps, 29 West Susquehanna Avenue, Suite 210, Baltimore, MD 21204

ICAD: an electronic mail network on the topic of abuse & disability. (Often deals with the issue of "programmatic abuses" and discusses alternatives.) Subscription is free. E-mail message to: majordomo@srv.ualberta.ca that reads SUBScribe icad. If any difficulty in subscribing contact dick_sobsey@.ualberta.ca

About Diverse City Press (514-297-3080)

Diverse City Press has set a goal of publishing vital, insightful, yet affordable material for people in the field of developmental disabilities. We are open to comments regarding our books and videos, we are also open to receiving manuscripts from individuals who work directly with people with developmental disabilities.

Other Products Available

The Psychiatric Tower of Babble: Understanding People with Developmental Disabilities who have Mental Illness, by Sue Gabriel

Just Say Know! Understanding and Reducing the Risk of Sexual Victimization of People With Developmental Disabilities, by Dave Hingsburger

Hand Made Love: Teaching about Male Masturbation through Understanding and Video, by Dave Hingsburger

Under Cover Dick: Teaching about Condom Use through Understanding and Video, by Dave Hingsburger

and coming next

Using Art as a Healing Tool for Individuals with Developmental Disabilities, by Cindy Caprio-Orsini (title may change)